Mandy Tuck

KONSEP BOOKS
KONSEP LAGENDA SDN BHD (223 855)
Kuala Lumpur 59100, MALAYSIA

Email: fengshui@lillian-too.com.
WEBSITE: www.lillian-too.com

LILLIAN TOO'S FLYING STAR FENG SHUI

ISBN 983 9778 - 72 - 2

First published as
CHINESE NUMEROLOGY IN FENG SHUI
In Dec 1994 and reprinted nine times
Fully updated and revised new edition January 1999
This second printing of new edition June 1999

Printed by Ritz Print S/B
Kuala Lumpur
Malaysia

LILLIAN TOO'S
FLYING STAR
FENG SHUI

This highly acclaimed book reveals the secrets of **time dimension** in feng shui.

Apply **Chinese Numerology** in FENG SHUI to predict good and bad periods in different parts of the home and office

Written by
LILLIAN TOO
the world's leading writer on Feng shui
in collaboration with
Grand Master
YAP CHENG HAI

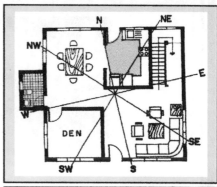

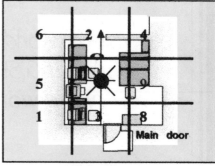

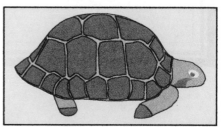

With love
for
JENNIFER

Visit the world's first completely online
FENG SHUI MAGAZINE at
www.worldoffengshui.com

Meet Lillian Too

From one book to the next, I go deeper and shui," says geomancy author **Lillian Too**. published volumes rises around the M plicity seems to be more her motif t years ago, she wrote the bestselli *Illustrated Guide to Feng Shui*. La: the *Feng Shui Fundamentals* sen year she published *Lillian Too's* Now, though, she really gets d bones with the release of *Lillia of Feng Shui*: bite-size morse for everyday life. Is it by desig works are more pared down? " demystify feng shui," she says books, I thought I made it eas come to me and say 'mak knows all about m complicated. she left her ecutive cl Kong de Dragor back t

From ASIAWEEK

She has become the world's number ONE selling writer on a subject that is taking the world by storm. Her books on Feng shui have penetrated every corner of the globe. She has made bestseller lists in USA, UK, Germany, Holland, Norway, South Africa, Australia, Malaysia and Singapore. In the UK, USA and in Singapore her books have reached number ONE in the Bestseller charts. Her **LITTLE BOOK OF FENG SHUI** was <u>number ONE in the UK Bestseller charts for four months</u> and is still on the lists and her sequel **LITTLE BOOK OF FENG SHUI AT WORK** has entered the charts ..

Her feng shui books have been **translated into sixteen languages** – German, French, Spanish, Greek, Italian, Polish, Japanese, Indonesian, Slovenian, Portuguese, Swedish, Russian, Norwegian, Czechoslovakian Hungarian, and (surprise !) Chinese. She has **sold well over a million copies of her** books worldwide and is constantly invited to speak on feng shui in five continents. In **Malaysia** where she comes from, Lillian Too is described by **Malaysian Business**, the country's leading business magazine as "... *Something of a legend in corporate circles being the first woman there to become the Managing Director of a publicly listed company* " Lillian is an MBA graduate from the **Harvard Business School,** in Boston USA; She has been characterized as being "*in a league of her own* " by **SUCCESS** magazine while the internationally acclaimed **VOGUE** describes her " *as someone people listen to..* Lillian Too is married and has one daughter.

PUBLISHED BY KONSEP LAGENDA SDN BHD

* Feng Shui * Applied Pa Kua Lo Shu Feng Shui
* Practical Applications of Feng Shui
* Water Feng Shui for Wealth
* Dragon Magic - my feng shui stories
* Feng Shui Good Fortune Symbols
* Chinese Astrology for Romance and Relationships
* Lillian Too's Basic Feng shui
* Lillian Too's Personalized Feng Shui Tips
* The Chinese Dragon * Strategies for Career Success
* Creative Visualization * Tap the Power Inside You
* Explore the Frontiers of your Mind

PUBLISHED BY ELEMENT BOOKS
U.K, Australia and USA
* **The Complete Illustrated Guide to Feng Shui.**
* FENG SHUI Fundamentals series of nine books:
* Feng shui in eight easy lessons;
* Feng shui for Love; * Feng shui for Education;
* Feng shui for Networking; * Feng shui for Career,
* Feng shui for Children; * Feng shui for Health;
* Feng shui for Fame; * Feng shui for Wealth.
The Complete Illustrated Guide to FENG SHUI for GARDENS
Lillian Too's Little Book of Feng Shui
Lillian Too's Little Book of Feng Shui at work

PUBLISHED BY RIDER BOOKS,
RANDOM HOUSE, UK
And BALLANTINE IN USA
* Feng Shui Essentials
* Creating Abundance with Feng shui

PUBLISHED BY COLLINS & BROWN,
LONDON, UK.
* Lillian Too's Easy To Use Feng shui - 168 ways to success

LILLIAN TOO'S FLYING STAR FENG SHUI

CONTENTS

What others say ....

" ... Too distills the essence of the practice and explains in simple terms how feng shui can improve anyone's life ..."
VOGUE magazine

" Too's credentials are impeccable"
SARAWAK SUNDAY TRIBUNE

" ... to the readers of her best selling books throughout Malaysia, Lillian Too has only just begun"
BUSINESS TIMES

" ... Lillian Too is something of a legend in Malaysian corporate circles ... with a formidable cv... " MALAYSIAN BUSINESS

" ... Too is a person who practices what she preaches "
NEW STRAITS TIMES

" ... she is not the sort of proponent of this ancient Chinese art who peddles her knowledge to companies ... what she does, and has done with considerable success, is write books about feng shui ... "
SMART INVESTOR

" Lillian Too's feng shui site has been big news. Feng shui is the Chinese art of geomancy - a cross between psychic energy and interior design - and Lillian Too can make a Swiss ski chalet seem as spiritual as Stonehenge ... in Asia she is a celebrity and her online consultations are burning up lots of Asian band - width ..."
WIRED, USA

" Highly readable and with interesting anecdotes, Lillian Too's FENG SHUI should interest everyone who seeks to understand the forces of Nature ... it is an invaluable addition to the growing literature on Eastern thinking and Lillian Too is to be congratulated for her timely contribution ... "
Dr Tarcisius Chin, CEO
MALAYSIAN INSTITUTE OF MANAGEMENT

What others say ....

... An interesting read
I found myself looking at my flat in a totally different way"
The OBSERVER newspaper London on
Lillian Too's FENG SHUI FUNDEMENTALS

... With great illustrations and clear explanations, Lillian Too demonstrates
how to make the best of our living spaces and offers plenty of tips to improve
energy flows immediately."
PREVIEW Magazine, UK gives
Lillian Too's FENG SHUI IN EIGHT EASY LESSONS
a five star rating.

This is a book to guide you through FENG SHUI's roots ... its principles and
practice ... how to harness energy lines and live in harmony with your
environment.
UK'S COUNTRY LIVING
on The Complete Illustrated Guide to Feng Shui ...

... Donald Trump, Olivia Newton John and Boy George have all had their
homes feng shui-ed by experts... BUT Lillian Too's Feng shui Kit
contains all you need to do it yourself.
The Saturday MIRROR, UK
on LILLIAN TOO'S FENG SHUI KIT

"Lillian Too's FENG SHUI is outstanding and spellbinding in more ways than
one. Here is a piece of work that has been well researched and represents
what the writer has "soaked up" from books and practitioners. The well
matched marriage between theory and practice contributes to the
comprehensiveness of the book. Yet there is no false pretensions on the part
of the writer ... the reader's interest is sustained throughout the book.
I highly recommend this book for both practitioners and non practitioners".

Professor Dr. Leong Yin Ching PhD (London)
Professor of Education UNIVERSITY OF MALAYA

The Science of FENG SHUI with LILLIAN TOO

www.lillian-too.com

Email

fengshui@lillian-too.com

Water over Wood,
The image of the Well ...
Thus the superior man
encourages the people at
their work
And exhorts them to help
one another.

**From the I CHING on the
Hexagram Ching**

Opening Notes ....

Fire over Wood,
The image of the Cauldron ...
Thus the superior man consolidates his fate
By making his position correct

**From the I CHING on the
Hexagram Ting**

OPENING
NOTES

SPACE
&
TIME
CONCEPTS
IN
FENG
SHUI

OPENING NOTES from the author

SPACE
& TIME CONCEPTS IN FENG SHUI

Feng shui influences have space and time concepts. Many of my earlier books on feng shui in this KONSEP series dealt almost exclusively with landscapes, directions and locations, which have to do with space dimensions. To make the practice of feng shui complete, the ancient texts refer also to the relevance of time cycles in feng shui. My first book on time cycles and the impact of the passage of time on feng shui was Chinese Numerology which directly addressed this concept.

This book is a revised new edition of that book renamed, more appropriately **FLYING STAR** feng shui to follow the exact Chinese translation of this technique of feng shui.

Flying Star feng shui focuses on the significance of changing forces during different time periods. The process highlights the intangible influences of the numbers and combinations of numbers of the magic **Lo Shu square.**

This adds vital nuances to "good" and "bad" feng shui and explaining that good luck or bad luck caused by harmony or disharmony in the environment does not necessarily occur continuously or last forever.

Nor do auspicious and inauspicious orientations stay so throughout one's entire lifetime.

Feng shui masters point to the rise and fall of Dynasties to give credence to their conviction that this time element in feng shui practice should not be ignored. Many therefore maintain that annual and periodic check of one's feng shui based on flying star methods are necessary.

**OPENING
NOTES**

SPACE
&
TIME
CONCEPTS
in
FENG
SHUI

OPENING NOTES   from the author ....

Flying Star feng shui allows the practitioner to undertake annual monitoring of changes in the feng shui luck of a house by studying the influence of the earth's intangible forces. This is Time dimension feng shui which therefore alerts the practitioner to inauspicious forces. Unless dealt with or countered these intangible forces can cause serious misfortune to befall residents. Equally also, there are auspicious forces and these too can be enhanced.

Acknowledging the efficacy of time dimension feng shui begs some questions. For instance if feng shui luck does change over time, how does one explain the extravagant claims of certain texts – particularly those that promise great wealth for present and future generations when specific feng shui conditions are met.

Surely, if as postulated by the advocates of the time dimension theory the feng shui characteristics of a dwelling or work place can and does change over time, then surely the feng shui attributes of an ancestral home would generate changing fortunes for future generations ?

There is also the question about feng shui for YIN dwellings. I am referring to the dwelling places for the ancestral dead – tombs, gravesites and burial grounds.

If the feng shui of burial places have been carefully designed to generate favourable conditions for descendants, a practice that is widespread in Taiwan and elsewhere, surely their fortunes will change when the time dimension of feng shui exert its cyclical influence ?

Surely prosperity and excellent good fortune in a family cannot last forever ? Perhaps it is this dimension of feng shui practice that has led to the widespread belief that family wealth rarely, if ever survives three generations.

I am persuaded that Time dimensions MUST be taken account of and that feng shui expertise cannot be complete without taking this aspect of its practice into account. When first introduced to the theories of time dimension feng shui, I was reminded of the fundamental philosophy of the **I Ching** – the source book of Chinese thought.

Subtitled " the Book of Changes" the I Ching expounds the Yin and Yang view of the Universe which has to do with balance in the environment and with the complementarity of the forces of Nature.

The I Ching declares that all good fortune contains tiny seeds of misfortune, and that likewise when times are bad they also embrace the seeds of good fortune. Like the cycles of earth, cycles of time exert their potent influence, which then lead to cycles of change – thus transforming good into bad and bad into good.

Viewed from such a perspective the philosophical underpinnings of the time dimension theory of feng shui would seem wholly consistent with this most basic tenet of the origins of feng shui ideology. Those presently suffering from bad times can therefore take heart that bad times do become better over time while those presently enjoying good fortune should guard against the incidence of over arrogance lest their good fortune dissipates.

I am also persuaded that the time dimension theory does not conflict with those that deal with spatial concepts on the subject, and that if anything time complements and gives meaning to space. Nothing is static. The earth is dynamic and ever changing.

Thus even while the guidelines on directions and locations based on either the landscape or compass schools offer powerful techniques on how to feng shui dwellings and work places, time dimension cannot be ignored. The time theory of feng shui does not contradict the laws of From School. Instead, it adds important complementary dimensions that give depth to the practice. Time concepts thus simply cannot be ignored.

This book serves to fill the gap. Flying Star feng shui as a method of computation seems complex but in reality is quite easy. It is in the interpretation of the numerals and their meanings that is not so easy to grasp or practice. I have tried to make sure that what is contained in this book is as simplified as possible. I have included Lo Shu Natal charts of all houses built in this current period of 7. Sufficiently so, to help the layman who wishes to obtain a working knowledge for personal use.

**OPENING
NOTES**

**SPACE
& TIME
CONCEPTS
in FENG
SHUI**

Numbers
& the
Lo Shu
Grid

OPENING NOTES *from the author ...*

Numbers and the Lo Shu Grid

Time dimension theory revolves around numbers and reflect the basic fundamentals of Chinese Numerology. The main tool in the formulation and understanding of this theory is the original Lo Shu square (shown below). In this square, the numbers one to nine are arranged around the nine squares of the Lo Shu grid in such a way that any three numbers add up to fifteen in any direction – whether calculated horizontally, vertically or diagonally. The number 15 express the number of days it takes for a moon's full waxing or waning cycle.

Even numbers which carry yin energy, are placed at each of the four corners of the square. Thus note the positions of the numbers, 2, 4, 6, and 8.

The yang **odd numbers** appear on the four compass points. Thus 1, 3, 7, and 9 are placed on north, east, west and south while the number 5 is placed in the center.

The numbers move around the gird in a pre set sequence which sets the flight path for the way all other numerals should "fly". These numbers have meanings. They signify the elements. They interact with each other and they interact significantly with the objects of the compass location where they are found.

These interactions are dynamic and they create the intangible unseen forces that transform the energy either into bad killing energy or into good lucky energy. How to diagnose the relevant combination of numbers in various locations of the home is what flying star feng shui is about. To understand flying star feng shui thus requires one to understand the meanings of these numbers. Then to interpret whether the numbers in each compass location bring good fortune or not and if not what to do to counter the bad effect of bad flying stars.

This method of diagnosing feng shui is known as **FEY SIN FENG SHUI or FLYING STAR FENG SHUI.** In actual fact of course, the stars that are referred to are imaginary stars. The imaginary main star numeral. The imaginary water star and the imaginary mountain star.

In each of the nine grids there is a **main star** numeral, a **mountain star** numeral and a **water star** numeral. These star numerals change (or fly) from one grid to the next. They also fly from period to period. Look at the example of a typical Lo Shu Flying star natal chart. This chart shows a period of 7 house with its main door located in the North sector and the door facing the first subsection of North direction.

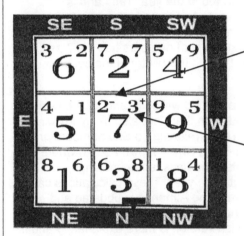

This is the chor sin or mountain star on the left hand side of the main star. All the numbers on the left are chor sin numerals.

This is the siang sin center star. All the small numbers on the right are siang sin stars.

Note how these secondary star numbers change as they move round the grid.

Flying star feng shui examines these star numerals and draw conclusions about auspicious and inauspicious sectors of a dwelling place during a specific time period based on these star numbers. The 'stars" together with the main numerals from 1 to 9 are said to move around the Lo Shu grid. Their pattern of movement follows the placement of numbers in the original Lo Shu Square with the numeral 5 in the center. Depending on how the numeral changes as they move into different sectors, the feng shui of a dwelling place may be diagnosed. This technique, its method of computation, its analyses and applications make up the substance of this book. When you become adept at flying star you would have mastered the only truly divinitive branch of feng shui practice. Flying star enables the Master practitioner to make reliable but generalized predictions about specific types of bad luck that can befall a house, a city or country. In Hong Kong there are Masters who can accurately predict the ups and downs of the stock Index. This feng shui can also predict economic swings pinpointing specific turning points of ups and downs.

OPENING
NOTES

SPACE
& TIME
CONCEPTS
in FENG
SHUI

REIGNING
NUMBERS

OPENING NOTES from the author ...

REIGNING NUMBERS AND TIME PERIODS

Flying star usage starts with the knowledge of time periods. The numbers of the Lo Shu square vary from period to period. In each period there is what is referred to as "the reigning Lo Shu number.

Presently we are in the period of 7 and this twenty year period started in the year 1984 and is scheduled to come to an end in the year 2003. The reigning number is 7 because the applicable Lo Shu arrangement of numbers has the 7 as the main numeral star in the center of the square.

The reigning number for the next 20 year period will be 8, and for the twenty year period following that will be 9. In addition there are also reigning stars for each year, each month and each day. These reigning Lo Shu numbers are an integral part of the Chinese Almanac or **Tung Shu** (shown above) where good and bad days for all sorts of events (weddings, shop openings, launchings etc) are specially worked out each year. These calculations can be said to be are based on flying star as well. The Almanac is updated and sold annually in countries in the Far East. The Chinese version has a very detailed listing of good and bad dates. The English version is more explanatory and is not a reference calendar in the way the Chinese version is.

NATAL CHART OF DWELLINGS

In addition, and more relevant to feng shui practice, these reigning numbers also form the basis for casting the natal chart of dwelling places, buildings, homes and any kind of structure. From the natal chart it is possible to tell whether any place or building in question will enjoy generally favourable feng shui or not during designated months and years. These periods of good or bad feng shui can be as short as a week or as long as the entire year. The natal chart also reveals the locations within a house that will have excellent luck during that period and the rooms that could cause illness, loss and serious misfortune. How to cast and read the natal chart is part of this book. The method is given, and for those who find that flying stars too complicated to comprehend, ready made charts have also been specially calculated. So that all that's needed is to undertake the interpretation of the stars.

Interpretation & Meanings

The chapters that discuss the interpretation and meanings of the numerals and combinations of numerals must be studied carefully. Note the meanings of the numbers are based on two significant symbolic relationships, ie.

- on the meanings of the numbers themselves and
- on the relationship between the numbers and the elements and then on the implied interaction of the five elements as expressed in the form of numbers. This dependence on the five elements or *Wuxing* is in actual fact the key to really understanding flying star.

The Five Elements

The Impact of **Wuxing** on flying star interpretation is extremely important. Usually the difference between "good" and "bad" feng shui masters is the depth of knowledge they each bring to bear when analyzing and interpreting the element relationships. This is because it is only when the understanding is correct, can the real remedies or enhancers be recommended. Also Wuxing is not as simple as it at first appears. The understanding of the Productive and Destructive Cycle is only the start in understanding Wuxing. The inter relationships is in actual fact a lot more complex.

The best feng shui Master is the one who truly understands the subtleties and nuances of the way the five elements are said to interact with each other. This will be the feng shui master who is able to advice on the best form of feng shui cure, antidote, enhancer or activator.

Each number from 1 to 9 represents an element.

But the exact nature of the representation differs from number to number. Thus for instance both 3 and 4 represent the wood element; but 3 is big wood and 4 is small wood.

More, 3 is Arousing wood while 4 is the Gentle wood. Also 3 is male and 4 is female and so on. Each of these attributes adds on a layer of meaning. The whole should then be viewed in entirety so that a coherent picture emerges. It is in implementing the combinations that good feng shui is achieved.

This presents the challenge to the practitioner. But it also makes the practice of flying star so exciting. This is because when you do get it absolutely right the good fortune comes almost immediately and it is **really like striking gold**

OPENING
NOTES

SPACE
& TIME
CONCEPTS
in FENG
SHUI

MEANINGS
Of
NUMBERS

OPENING NOTES   from the author ...

Other Meanings of Numbers

The numbers also have meanings in accordance to the corresponding trigram. These operate at two levels.

- One, the symbolic relationship between number and trigram is at the start based on the placement of the numbers in the original Lo Shu square.
- Second, when interpreting natal chart and period Lo Shu flying charts we also have to see the relationship of the numbers in the period flying chart under review. Thus for example the number 1 is representative of the trigram Kan in the original Lo Shu square. Then in a flying start chart for say this year (1999), the number 1 has flown into the center. This means Kan which represents water has flown into the center, which is of the earth element ... according to conventional analysis water coming to earth does not harm the earth unless it comes in, in large amounts. Thus we will need to combine this reading with the actual natal chart of the house. If there is a preponderance of 1's in the center grid and especially if the water star is also 1 in the center grid then we are looking at an excess of water in the center. This spells a situation of danger.

These symbolic relationships form the basis of Chinese Numerology interpretations. It is important to appreciate the subtleties of the five elements. Feng shui is usually not just about each element or number being bad or good. It is also about the "**heaviness**" of the occurrence of the number. When there is excess of anything, there ceases to be harmony and balance. And when disharmony rules the feng shui has become sour.

Readers who wish to proceed further in their study of feng shui interpretations to supplement and indeed, improve their practical knowledge and experience can supplement their study with readings from the I Ching. This ancient classic will reveal profound wisdoms that will deepen anyone's understanding of how earth energy works and how the natural landscapes are affected by subtle energy flows that mirror that of the winds and the waters.

It is with this in mind that I have collected some of the more thought provoking statements of the I Ching and scattered them through this book as captions to accompany exquisite brush paintings of landscape. The I Ching's references to superior men, apply equally to the feminine gender, and couched in these references are subtle pieces of advice that accompany the judgement and images of the particular trigram or hexagram. If you think through these quotations you will catch a glimpse of the I Ching's perspective on man's living condition with that of the earth.

OPENING NOTES   from the author ...

My books on feng shui represent a very small and humble adjunct of the wisdoms extracted from the great Book of Changes. It is now over twenty years since I discovered the I Ching. It is a book that never ceases to amaze me. In my attempts to understand the ideologies expounded within the pages of this classic, I have been helped along by many experts and scholars who collectively and separately opened my eyes to deeper levels of meanings expounded by the hexagrams of the I Ching. This greatly expanded my perceptions of the mysterious forces that shape the energy lines of Nature. I derive a great deal of satisfaction to be able to pass on many of these collective insights and tenets through my books, as much to share the knowledge as to raise conscious awareness of these particular ingredients in the whole spectrum of feng shui knowledge and practice.

These Opening notes were first written in 1994 when I published this book under the title Chinese Numerology in Feng shui. Today five years later, feng shui has gained so much acceptance and popularity globally, it astounds me. At that time I had used flying star divination to investigate if my books on feng shui (three of which shown here) would succeed in penetrating the worldwide market. I also asked the I Ching if I would succeed in my quest to raise awareness of this wonderful practice worldwide.

The I Ching predicted for me a worldwide explosion of interest in feng shui – *like thunder, the sound can be heard a thousand li*, it predicted ....Today, five years later ... I have become internationally known through my books on feng shui and the subject itself has spawned over 200 books and over 168 websites on the worldwide web.

Total sales of all my 23 books are now close to 1.3 million copies worldwide. The I Ching has predicted that interest in feng shui will continue to grow for 18 years after which it will plateau and be as common as astrology and other similar subjects.

OPENING
NOTES

SPACE
& TIME
CONCEPTS
in FENG
SHUI

Many
feng shui
Masters

OPENING NOTES   from the author ...

In the West – in Europe, UK, Australia, USA and Canada and in South America and South Africa – feng shui has become a popular main stream subject. It has captured the imagination of many readers.

One of the best things which has resulted from this explosion of positive interest is the emergence now of many truly authentic masters of feng shui. They are immigrant Chinese who live in different parts of the world but already many of them, have been inspired by the appreciation of their knowledge to now come out to reveal their secrets and their knowledge. As a result the worldwide practice of feng shui will be considerably enhanced as knowledge gets shared.

If you want to read about the development of feng shui worldwide you might like to visit the Internet's first online FENG SHUI MAGAZINE. The website address is at:

www.worldoffengshui.com

Feng shui is an ancient science with exciting applications for modern living. It has brought me huge good luck and it can do the same for you.
Please enjoy your investigation into this wonderful science ....

 Lillian Too
January 1999

The earth's condition is receptive
The superior man who has breath of character
Carries the outer world ...
From the I CHING on the Trigram KUN

Chapter One
Basic Symbols and Cycles of Time

The wind drives over the water
The superior man sets his calendar in order
And makes the seasons clear ...

From the I CHING on the Trigram HUAN

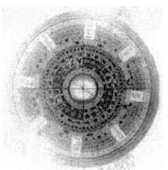

All divinitive sciences associated with Chinese numerology have their origins in the nine sector Lo Shu grid. To practitioners of feng shui, this grid is regarded as a magic square whose arrangement of the numbers one to nine, possess certain mystical connotations that reflect the way energy lines move along the earth's surfaces.

Some of these energy lines create brilliantly potent flows of auspicious luck, while others cause deadly circulations of bad luck - what the Chinese refer to as the dragon's cosmic breath, the good breath *sheng chi*, and the pernicious killing breath *shar chi*, respectively.

Hence, the Lo Shu square is regarded as the key that unlocks much of the mysteries surrounding the interpretation of feng shui formulas particularly to the way they affect the cosmic breath..

In this connection it is useful to remember that feng shui science comprise of two major schools - the landscape school (which takes its cue from the way landforms and waterways affect one's dwelling place), and the compass school, which focuses more directly on the influences of compass directions.)

There is another way to approach the practice of feng shui, i.e. to view it as having a space concept, and a time concept. Physical landforms and objects that have a tangible form influence spatial feng shui. Time concept on the other hand deal with intangible forces that are invisible to the naked eye. They are nevertheless no less potent.

CHAPTER
ONE

BASIC
SYMBOLS
&
CYCLES
OF TIME

Basic symbols & cycles of time

ONE

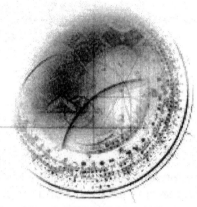

Abstract forces that are based on the intangible influences of numbers, their combinations and their symbolic relationships influence time dimension feng shui. It is thus very different from physical landscape feng shui.

Time dimension feng shui requires the drawing up of a special chart which discloses the placement of various numbers (or *stars* as they are generally referred to in the ancient formulas). These placements are such that each number, or set of numbers correspond to one of the eight cardinal or secondary directions of the compass. It is from this chart that time dimension feng shui is then diagnosed for a house or building. The computation of the numbers around this chart follows the set up of the numbers around the basic (or original) Lo Shu square. This original square has the number 5 in the center. This method is called the Flying Star method of feng shui.

The first step in using flying star is to learn how to cast these charts which are known as <u>natal charts</u>. These charts comprise numbers placed around the eight different directions (and the center) as laid out in the nine sectors of the Lo Shu grid. In addition to their intrinsic meanings, these numbers also express manifestations of the symbols associated with the mysterious trigrams (three lined symbols originating from the ancient I Ching) that are placed around the eight sided Pa Kua.

The investigation of time dimension feng shui therefore requires an intensive re look at the basic symbols which impact on the numerology computations and interpretations. This means that the nuances and subtleties of the meanings attached to the various symbols of the Pa Kua (including the five elements, the members of the family, the seasons, the colours and so forth) should be understood as clearly as possible.

Only then can there be meaningful and substantial depth applied to the interpretations of the numbers when attempting to construe their meanings. Without correct interpretations, the novice practitioner could inadvertently make mistakes that could well have been avoided.

Those of you already familiar with my second book on Pa-Kua Lo-Shu feng shui would already have been introduced to KUA numbers. These KUA numbers are the same as the numbers referred to in the flying star formula. But the KUA numbers have no inputs in the interpretations of flying star. Flying star numbers refer to the entire house while KUA numbers are relevant for individuals.

The main numeral that is placed in the center of the Lo Shu square is the number that has been designated to apply to periods - days, months and years - in a fixed formula or pattern. Using these numbers one is able to apply different applications of the flying star formula which feng shui masters use in their practice.

These numbers are the same as the **reigning numbers** of periods for the Flying Star school of feng shui.

In this book, rather than go through the laborious process of explaining how these numbers have been worked out for each of the different periods, the respective reigning numbers have already been computed. Readers need only refer to the relevant sections on reigning numbers to extract the numbers required for drawing up the numerology natal charts for their homes or buildings.

Remember that the reigning numbers are the key to investigating the feng shui of your home/building during a specified period.

CHAPTER
ONE

BASIC
SYMBOLS
&
CYCLES
OF TIME

The LO
SHU
Square

Basic symbols & cycles of time	ONE

THE LO SHU MAGIC SQUARE

According to documented legend, a noble tortoise emerged from the River Lo, sometime around 2205 BC (about 4000 years ago), carrying on its huge back, special and significant markings which the ancients interpreted as the primary numbers, one to nine.

THE **LO SHU** SQUARE with the numbers 1 to 9 arranged in sequence.

The **PA KUA** with the later heaven sequence of TRIGRAMS

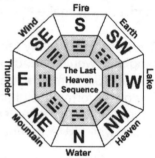

These numbers appeared in the form of circular dots, and were arranged in a three by three nine grid pattern. The pattern of numbers were arranged in such a way that adding any three numbers in a straight line in whatever direction - horizontally, vertically or diagonally - made up a total of 15, which coincided with the number of days in each of the 24 phases of the solar year. These pattern of numbers with the number 5 placed in the center is shown in the series of diagram above.

The three grid pattern also corresponded to the eight sides of the Pa Kua, around a ninth central point and this pattern of numbers soon became irretrievably associated with the eight Trigrams of the Pa-Kua, in particular, the Trigrams as arranged according to the Later Heaven Sequence as shown above. The pattern of numbers came to be known as the Lo Shu magic square, and in time, this square came to exert a powerful and mythical influence on Chinese cultural symbolism.

Lo Shu symbolism also extended connections between the numbers and the <u>Four Celestial Animals</u> - the **Dragon, the Tiger, the Tortoise** and the **Phoenix** - as well as with the Five Elements - Fire, Earth, Water, Wood and Metal. In time the Lo Shu grid became the foundation of Taoist magical practice and many of Taoism's rituals continue to be synchronized in accordance with the Lo Shu pattern and arrangement of numbers.

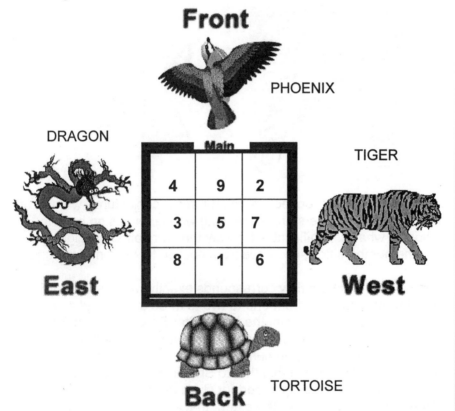

Lo Shu "magic" features strongly and significantly in all the Compass I formulas and theories of feng shui. Indeed, the square is perceived to contain the "key" to unlocking the mysterious secrets of many of these theories. The above diagram illustrates the relationship between the odd yang numbers 1,3,7 and 9 with the four celestial creatures. Thus note that 3 is dragon and 7 is tiger. That I is the tortoise and 9 is the phoenix.

CHAPTER
ONE

BASIC
SYMBOLS
&
CYCLES
OF TIME

The LO
SHU
Square

Basic symbols & cycles of time | ONE

Some scholars have written about the striking similarities they discern between the Lo Shu's arrangement of numbers, with that of the potent symbols of other cultures, in particular the ancient Hebrew Cultures whose reputedly powerful Saturnic sign - the **"Sigil of the planet Saturn"** - is similar, in its "movement" or flow, to that of the Lo Shu. This is illustrated in the series of diagrams below.

 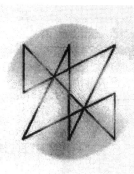

While much of this "connection" must remain conjecture - we are, after all attempting to understand something whose origins go back to antiquity, what is significant is the way the correlation highlights the way the numbers flow, i.e. move from section to section of the square.

The way the numbers flow corresponds exactly with the Sigil of Saturn! This flow of numbers - from one to two to three to four and so on ... along the grid is the basis of the Flying Star School of Feng Shui! As we shall see later on when we study the formula in greater detail, the arrangement of the Lo Shu numbers seem to exert some mysterious power. It is very possible that the Lo Shu arrangement of numbers holds the key to unlocking important clues regarding the true workings of the forces of Nature. To the extent that as the numbers move, they somehow reflect the changing moods and influences of these forces - thereby encapsulating the important transformations of yin into yang and vice versa.

Whatever the explanations, it remains an irrefutable fact that the basic Lo Shu square is at the center of feng shui's most powerful formulas. One of these formulas has already been covered in depth in my other formula book, Applied Pa Kua and Lo Shu Feng Shui.

THE PA-KUA LO-SHU RELATIONSHIP

The diagram on the right illustrates the relationship between the eight-sided Pa Kua and the Nine grid Lo Shu magic square. Readers will note that the Pa-Kua shown here places the direction of South at the top, to correspond with the number 9.

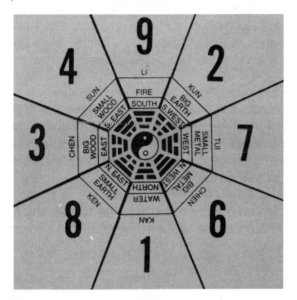

This is because the Chinese compass places south at the top, and to ensure consistency and accuracy, it is necessary when relationships between symbols are being analyzed, to comply with the practice followed in the ancient manuals. For practical purposes, however, readers may use modern compasses, which place north at the top. However, it is vital that mistakes should not be made when attempting to conceive interpretations based on symbolic relationships between numbers and the Trigrams.

Readers will also note that the arrangement of the eight Trigrams in this Pa-Kua is based on the Later Heaven Sequence. This is because all latter day practice of both Chinese Astrology and Chinese Feng Shui adopt this sequential representation of the Pa Kua's Trigrams. Much of the Ganzhi system of Heavenly stems and Earthly branches also correlate to this Later Heaven Sequence.

CHAPTER
ONE

BASIC
SYMBOLS
&
CYCLES
OF TIME

Later and
Early
Heaven
Pa Kua

Basic symbols & cycles of time | ONE

Feng Shui Masters also generally use this Pa-Kua sequential arrangement when diagnosing the feng shui of Yang dwelling places i.e. the homes and work places of the living - (as opposed to those of the dead - i.e. graveyards and burial grounds).

This is based on the belief that the Later Heaven Arrangement is:
- closer to the attributes to life on Earth
- is a closer approximation to the natural forces of Nature, and
- more accurately reflects the harmony and intrinsic balances of the seasons of the year and the cycles of time.

The distinction between "Early" and "Later" Heaven Arrangements of the Pa-Kua's Trigrams is vital for the correct practice of feng shui since the placement of the Trigrams around the Pa-Kua are drastically different under the two arrangements. The application of the feng shui method dealt with in this book is based totally on the Later Heaven Arrangement of the Pa-Kua.

From the diagram on the previous page the relationships between the nine numbers of the Lo-Shu and the Trigrams can be summarized in the table below:

NUMBER	TRIGRAM	DIRECTION
9	LI	SOUTH
8	KEN	NORTHEAST
7	TUI	WEST
6	CHIEN	NORTHWEST
5	CENTER	CENTER
4	SUN	SOUTHEAST
3	CHEN	EAST
2	KUN	SOUTHWEST
1	KAN	NORTH

The relationship between the Lo Shu Numbers and the Pa Kua Trigrams (and their corresponding directions) has important implications later when we start to diagnosis the influence of the "flying stars" on the feng shui of a house.

The first thing to LEARN to do when attempting to apply feng shui formulas to one's house, is to learn to superimpose the Lo Shu symbol correctly onto one's house plan by identifying the compass directions of one's house and then matching them to those of the Lo shu numbers. This requires the house to be accurately subdivided in to nine grids to mirror the Lo-Shu grids. By then matching or fitting the directions, it is possible to identify the relevant Lo-Shu numbers of each of the sectors of the house. From then on, it is a simple enough matter to analyze the "*attributes*" of each of the sectors against the readings of the natal chart.

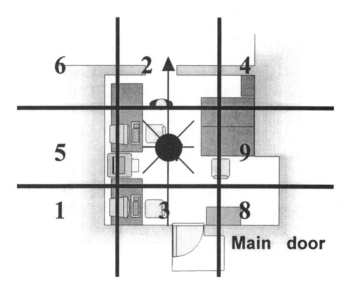

The example above shows a fairly regular shaped apartment that lends itself easily to the Lo Shu grid being superimposed onto it for analysis. Most homes are rarely so easy to cope with since there will be irregular shapes, missing corners and protruding extensions to cope with. As long as any part of the home is connected to the main house it must be inside the grid. Thus garages that stick out of a regular shaped house results in the house becoming "*irregular*" in shape with missing corners. Where there are other buildings near the house, as long as it is not connected with a continuous roofline, these extensions are deemed to be outside the grid.

CHAPTER
ONE

BASIC
SYMBOLS
&
CYCLES
OF TIME

The
Symbols of
the
PA KUA

Basic symbols & cycles of time | **ONE**

THE SYMBOLS OF THE PA-KUA

The Pa-Kua is full of symbols, and these assert significant influence on the way feng shui can be enhanced, or destroyed. The practice of feng shui has a great deal to do with correct interpretations of these symbols and their inter-relationships. The first steps in diagnosing and practicing feng shui therefore involves a study of the symbols, and from there extend the study towards:

a) The attributes of each of the Trigrams.
b) Relationships of the Trigrams to each other.
c) Interactions of the elements "assigned" to each Trigram.
d) Analyzing all of the above to the Numbers as they "*move*".

THE TRIGRAM LI corresponds to the direction <u>South</u>. The number is 9. It signifies the element of Fire. It represents brightness, the sun, lightning and the middle daughter. Its season is summer, and its is signified by the colour red. In feng shui, South is regarded a favourable direction because it represents warmth.

THE TRIGRAM KAN corresponds to the direction <u>North</u>. The number is 1. It signifies the element Water. Kan represents danger, the cold wind and the middle son. Its season is winter and its colour is black or dark blue. In feng shui, North is not generally considered an auspicious direction.

THE TRIGRAM CHEN corresponds to the direction East. The number is 3. It signifies the element big or heavy Wood. Its color is green and it represents the eldest son. Its image is thunder. Its season is spring. In feng shui, the East represents the abode of the celestial Green Dragon.

THE TRIGRAM TUI corresponds to the direction West. The number is 7. It signifies the element small Metal. It is also the representation of the youngest daughter or any young woman living in the household. In feng shui, West is the abode of the White Tiger. We are presently in the period of 7 therefore making this an auspicious number.

THE SYMBOLS OF THE PA-KUA

THE TRIGRAM SUN corresponds to the direction South East. The number is 4. Its element is small wood. It is also the representation of the eldest daughter. It is the wind and it means "penetrating" and "gentleness". Under certain schools of feng shui, its direction and sector represent wealth prospects.

THE TRIGRAM KUN embodies the Yin principle. It represents the matriarch, the cow, fertility, Mother earth and all things female. The number is 2. KUN must be activated by CHIEN to be productive. This sector represents marriage prospects in certain feng shui schools.

THE TRIGRAM KEN denotes the youngest son, small earth, keeping still, a period of waiting. The number is 8. KEN also signifies the successful pursuit of knowledge, and thus the direction - the Northeast - is conducive to study and research work.

THE TRIGRAM CHIEN embodies the Yang principle. It represents the patriarch, the father, the leader, and all things strong and enduring. CHIEN is the Northwest. The number is 6. It is Creative and it represents power and perseverance. Its element is metal, and for feng shui purposes one attribute of this sector is the presence of patrons, mentors and influential people in one's life.

The attributes of the Trigrams (and their corresponding directions and elements) must be factored into any analyses of the intangible forces of feng shui affecting any house or building. In respect of the flying star method, which investigates the time aspects of feng shui energies, it is absolutely necessary to understand the attributes of the eight Trigrams. By doing so it is possible to know which and how to activate the different directional sectors of one's house or building in order either to tap auspicious forces or to suppress negative influences.

CHAPTER
ONE

BASIC
SYMBOLS
&
CYCLES
OF TIME

The
Period
Cycles

Basic symbols & cycles of time

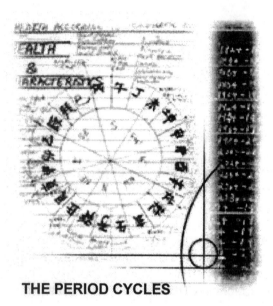

THE PERIOD CYCLES

The Upper Period
Reigning number 1
1864 to 1883
Reigning number 2
1884 to 1903
Reigning number 3
1904 to 1923
The Middle Period
Reigning number 4
1924 to 1943
Reigning number 5
1944 to 1963
Reigning number 6
1964 to 1983
The Lower Period
Reigning number 7
1984 to 2003
Reigning number 8
2004 to 2023
Reigning number 9
2024 to 2043

According to Chinese belief, there are Feng Shui period cycles of time, with each cycle lasting 180 years and each period lasting 20 years. Thus each cycle of time comprise 9 periods of 20 years each. (Thus 9 X 20 = 180). Why nine?

Because there are nine numbers in the Lo Shu magic square.

In each of these periods of 20 years, there is a <u>reigning number</u>. This assigned number, from 1 to 9, is placed in the center of the Lo-Shu square for purposes of feng shui analysis.

From the placement of this reigning number, the remaining numbers are then allotted their "*place*" in the grid based on the sequence of numbers in the original Lo-Shu square.

The analyses of how the numbers of the grid react with the placement of entrances within buildings create the intangible feng shui forces that enable the practitioner to chart the auspicious and inauspicious directions and sectors of a house or building during the particular period of time that is being investigated.

| Basic symbols & cycles of time | ONE |

THE REIGNING NUMBERS OF PERIODS
The numbers of the reigning periods will enable the practitioner to draw up the natal charts of buildings, houses, cities, and even countries for feng shui analyses.

The reigning number of every twenty years, gives its name to that period. For example we are now in the Period of 7. Because the origin of these numbers lie in the mysterious mathematical arrangements of the Lo-Shu and is influenced by the Pa-Kua, it is widely believed by feng shui masters that this number, i.e. the number that "rules" the period is extremely auspicious during the period. The number 7 therefore represent prosperity and wealth creation. For the current period therefore, the number 7 is regarded as an auspicious number which brings good fortune, and it will continue to be a lucky number until the end of the period - i.e. the year 2003. If this number is incorporated into a car number, a telephone number, a bank account number, a house number or any other personal number, it is believed to bring good luck.

As we have also seen earlier, it is possible to co-relate each of these numbers (except the center number 5) with the Trigrams of the Pa-Kua.

The association is based on the placement of the numbers in the original Lo-Shu, and their relationship with the Pa-Kua Trigrams based on the Later Heaven Arrangement. On the basis of this association between the numbers and the Trigrams it is possible to describe certain characteristics that lend themselves to interpretations for the periods. Thus, with respect to the periods of interest to readers, i.e. the periods 7,8,9, and 6 the following observations may be incorporated to later analyses when we study the time dimensions of feng shui under the flying star method.

THE PERIOD 7 corresponds to the Trigram TUI which represents, among other things, the direction West, the element metal, or gold, a young girl, a lake, the mouth, young children, and most of all, it represents joyousness. Some say the rise of women and of the importance of communication during this period (since1984) are manifestations of the period of 7 attributes.

CHAPTER
ONE

BASIC
SYMBOLS
&
CYCLES
OF TIME

The
Period
of 7 and 8

Basic symbols & cycles of time

... The period of 7

TUI (7) stands for things spiritual loosely categorized under the Mind, Body and Spirit rise of consciousness. Feng shui practitioners point to the emergence of young women in the professions and into leadership positions. They remind us of the popularity of the New Age and other neo spiritual revivals, related to the mouth - singing, speaking - the TV and media growth, as all due to the influences of the period 7.

The popularity of feng shui itself is a manifestation of the period 7's influence.

THE PERIOD 8

comes in 2004. It corresponds to the Trigram KEN. It represents the direction Northeast. Its element is earth and it signifies keeping still, like the mountain. KEN also personifies a young man and the Trigram is associated with the end of everything joined to a new beginning.
For purposes of feng shui the number 8 thus represents near future prosperity.
In terms of numbers the combination of **7** with **8** signifies great good fortune because it means current as well as future prosperity. Moreover it is significant that the element of 7 is metal and that of 8 is earth.

Because earth produces metal the element relationships is also in harmony thereby strengthening the combination of numbers.

THE PERIOD 9

Corresponds to the Trigram Li and it represents fire and lightning. This period will not come round until the year 2024. Thus for feng shui time analysis, the number 9 represents **distant prosperity**. Thus 9 does not have the immediacy of the number 8. However, because 9 is itself regarded as a very good and auspicious number, representing as it does the fullness of the Universe, the period of nine which is the period between 2024 to 2043 is regarded as a period that promises extremely bright prosperity.

THE PERIOD 6

Corresponds to the Trigram CHIEN and this is the period which has just passed. It began in 1964 and ended in 1983. The number six thus stands for **past prosperity**. However the number 6 is always regarded as a very auspicious number for the breadwinner of any household. Its Trigram belongs to the metal element and it represents the patriarch, a strong man, energy, power, brightness, endurance and perseverance.

The symbolism and characteristics suggested provide useful background knowledge for the practitioner especially in analyzing buildings and houses that were built during the period of 6.

Chapter Two
Flying Star Feng Shui

Within the earth, wood grows
The superior man of devoted character
Heaps up small things to achieve something high and great...

From the I CHING on the Trigram SHENG

Flying Star FENG SHUI

This school of feng shui - called *Fey Sin* or Flying Star method of feng shui, enables a practitioner to investigate auspicious and inauspicious corners and sectors of any house or building during the present twenty year fey sin period. The computation involves investigating the arrangement of numbers within the nine squares of the Lo-Shu grid, for the relevant month or year under investigation.

Here is a typical **Flying Star Natal chart** of a house built in the period of 7, thus the center number is 7. It looks complicated but is really very easy once you learn to identify the three star numerals – the main star, the siang sin star and the chor sin star. Then take note of the three numbers in each grid. These numbers have meanings which reveal the flying star analysis.

The analyses derived from the arrangement of numbers require the practitioner to understand the <u>movement of the *main star numerals*</u>, as well as that of the two secondary stars that are placed to the right and left of the main star numerals. The secondary star on the right is known as the ***siang sin*** or direction star, while the secondary star on the left of the main star numeral is known as the ***chor sin*** or sitting star. From there on, one must carefully examine the exact placements of all the star numerals (i.e. in which direction or sector of the building these stars are located.) This enables the practitioner to first discover which are the good and bad sectors in a house during any time period, and secondly, to see if the auspicious locations in the house are being occupied to tap the excellent feng shui and to their advantage. For instance whether the sector with the entrance (main door) is auspicious or not during a particular month, year or period. And if it is what can be done to magnify the good luck and when it is not, what can be done to counter the bad stars. This is the crux of the flying star feng shui. The intangible influences of the time dimension can be measured and acted upon to improve the feng shui of any building. Once one knows which corner of a home has good or bad "luck" during a certain time, it is possible to take measures to activate the good luck sectors and suppress the bad luck sectors.

CHAPTER
TWO

Flying Star
FENG
SHUI

The
Method

Flying Star FENG SHUI

TWO

Before starting, it is useful to fully understand the scope of the flying star technique. This method of feng shui is an advanced way of investigating the luck of a house or building by first **casting the natal chart** of the home. This is the first step in the process of flying star divination. Once you have the natal chart of any house or building, you will then be able to analyze it in the light of the " flying stars" of different periods. The forecasting aspect comes in because you can actually analyze your natal chart to see what the luck of the house will be this year, next year and every year in the future!

You can in effect use the natal chart to investigate the luck of any sector or room in the house as well. To take it further, using flying star you can also analyze the luck of a city or a country if you are skilled enough to work out the natal chart of the city based on its "date of birth" or a country based on when the country was " born" This is a trcky proposition, since it is not exactly easy to pinpoint exactly when a country is "born" For Malaysia of course I would put it as the date of our Independence ie 31st August 1957.

COMPUTING THE NATAL CHART
Computation must be done correctly. If the computation of the star numerals is not done correctly, the analyses will be flawed to the extent that serious mistakes can result. This can sometimes lead to dire consequences. To ensure accuracy of the practice therefore, the explanation of the steps in the computation is illustrated with two specific examples of computation.

<u>Step one</u>: First determine the period when your house was built OR when it was last renovated. Thus if your house was built in 1946 that makes it a period 5 house (see page 24) and the starting point is a Lo shu grid with the main numeral 5 in the center. However if it was extensively renovated say in 1975, this renovation will transform it into a period 6 house and then the main numeral in the center will be the one with the number 6. So the first step is selecting the Lo shu grid that applies to your house. If your house was built in 1990 or renovated in 1990 for example then you are living in a period of 7 house and the Lo shu grid to use is the one with the number 7 in the center.

A Period of **5** Lo shu Square. This is also the original Lo Shu Square. If your house was built between the years 1944 to 1963 or if this was the time when it was last renovated then to cast your natal chart you should use this Lo Shu square with this sequence of main numerals in the various sectors to get started. If however your house was renovated after 1963 you will have to move on to the next Lo shu square.

This is a period of **6** Lo Shu square. Note the number 6 in the center of the square. Because the number in the center has changed all the other numbers also change. It is useful for you to see how the numbers change because this charts the flight of the numbers .. ie how 5 becomes 6, and 6 becomes 7 and so forth. Once you familiarize yourself with the "flight" of the numbers, you will start to discern the pattern of the movement.

This is the period of 7 Lo Shu square. The number in the center has become 7 and again as a result of this all the numbers in the other grids of the square has also changed. This is the Lo Shu to use for all houses built or renovated between 1984 and 2003. This makes this also the Lo Shu of THIS period. We are now in the period of 7 and this makes 7 an auspicious number.

CHAPTER
TWO

Flying Star
FENG
SHUI

What
counts as
renovation

Flying Star FENG SHUI

TWO

When you are deciding between which Lo Shu square is the correct one to use, you might be fazed by the term "renovation". Not all feng shui masters agree on what constitutes a renovation. Certain flying star experts have indicated to me that only a major renovation that involves the addition of rooms or the changing of the entire roof with a lot of banging and building qualifies as a renovation in flying star analysis. This is the kind of renovation that is strong enough to change the flying star period and hence the Lo Shu square center numeral.

Other Masters insist that a repainting and change in the soft furnishings of the house will be sufficient to count as a renovation. Personally I believe this is a matter of personal judgement. For me, I do not consider a repaint and interior décor job a renovation. But I do not think one has to change the roofline for there to be sufficient building and construction to qualify for the term renovation. As long as there is banging, drilling, tearing down of walls and rebuilding of some parts of the house should count as renovation. Thus if you have done something like this to your house anytime from 1984 to the present then, irrespective of when your house was built, yours will qualify as a period of 7 house, and the main star numeral in the center will be 7. This will be your starting point.

Step Two: The next step is to determine the location and direction of the main door. Be very correct when determining which of the 8 sectors of your house the main door is located. To do this correctly you should superimpose the Lo-Shu Square onto your house plan. Having found the location of the main door you should then take the direction it faces out. This must be done as accurately as possible and therefore please use a good compass. Also, measure the dimensions of your house accurately so that the sectors get divided into squares as meticulously and accurately as possible.

You should take the direction three times on a good western compass. Stand just inside the house, then three feet inside and then 15 feet inside to take the direction. All three directions taken will be different. It is quite normal for there to be a some variance in the three readings. Use the average of the three directions to get it accurate.

TAKING DIRECTIONS

You will find that it pays to invest in a good reliable compass to take the compass orientations of your home. Learn how to use the compass. It is unnecessary to use the Luo Pan. Most feng shui practitioners cannot really understand more than a few rings of the FENG SHUI compass, and I have to say I am one of those people. I daresay some feng shui consultants pretend to read this compass to seem more authentic. In truth it is really not necessary because all you need is a good compass.

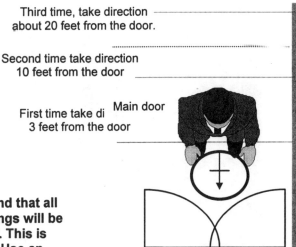

Third time, take direction about 20 feet from the door.

Second time take direction 10 feet from the door

First time take di   Main door
3 feet from the door

You will find that all three readings will be different. This is normal. Use an average of all three readings.

Also, it is **not** necessary to change the directions for flying star to work in the Southern Hemisphere. So if you are living in Australia, South America or South Africa, everything that is written in this book (and in all my other books) apply equally well in your Southern Hemisphere countries.

Do not listen to those who would have you believe otherwise. It is also not necessary to be confused by such people. They have their own agenda. Remember that feng shui is a practice that is not based on the western scientific tradition and to attempt to explain or alter the practice of feng shui using western scientific basis is like mixing apples with oranges.

CHAPTER
TWO

Flying Star
FENG
SHUI

Examples

Flying Star FENG SHUI

TWO

Examples to illustrate

Shown on this page is the Lo-Shu square of two different houses .

- **House A** has the front door located in the East and facing East
- **House B** has the door located in the Southwest and facing Southwest.

Note:

Both of these houses are period of 7 houses so that both have the main numeral 7 placed in the center. The **main star numerals** of House A and House B are illustrated below.

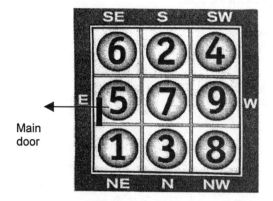

Main door

HOUSE A
The main door is located in the East and is also facing East

Main door

HOUSE B
The main door is located in the Southwest and is also facing Southwest. (Please note that it is perfectly acceptable for purposes of analysis to "rotate" the Lo Shu square to the left to make the analysis simpler.)

STEP THREE:
The next step is to determine the locations of the **chor sin star** and the **siang sin star** (expressed in numbers) in each of the compass sectors. This is done by first determining what number represents the chor sin and what number represents the siang sin in the center of the square. In our example, we are using the Lo-Shu, which applies to the period of 7, so the number 7 is in the center. The chor sin and siang sin are the little numbers that are placed on the left and right of this number. To familiarize yourself with this sequence look at the illustration on the following page. See if you can spot the chor sin star and the siang sin star.

But first let us get back to the Lo-Shu square with the number 7 in the center. From the diagram here you can see how the arrangement of numbers look. You will notice that this arrangement of numbers is different from the original Lo-Shu, which had the number 5 in the center. The placement of all the numbers in the eight sectors around the center also changes i.e. they have "*moved*" - but please note that they have not moved in a haphazard manner. The numbers in the Lo-Shu with 7 in the center have merely moved according to the order in the original Lo-Shu. You can work this "movement" out carefully by comparing the numbers in the original Lo-Shu - also reproduced here - with that of the No. 7 Lo-Shu. This movement is what gave rise to the term *flying* stars.

Original Lo Shu of 5

The flight path

Lo Shu of 7

The diagram of arrows in the center shows how the numerals mover from one grid to another. Thus note 4,5,6 is the center arrow in the Lo Su of 5 and it becomes 6,7,8 in the Lo Shu of 7.

CHAPTER
TWO

Flying Star
FENG
SHUI

Chor Sin
&
Siang Sin

Flying Star FENG SHUI | **TWO**

In our examples:

- **House A** where the main door was determined to be in the direction East, you can see that in the period of 7, the ruling number of the sector east is 5.
- **House B** we have noted that the main door is in the direction Southwest, and again in the period of 7, the ruling number of the sector southwest is the number 4.

These numbers offer vital clues to the quality of the feng shui of the house because these numbers determine the placement of the chor sin star and the siang sin star. Once the numbers of these two little stars are determined, it is possible to see what the three numerals of the center grid are. The feng shui "quality" of these three numbers has a bearing on the feng shui luck of the house, and in fact analysis of the flying star natal chart begins with these three center numbers.

STEP FOUR:
The next step is to determine the center numbers of the chor sin and the siang sin. These are the secondary stars of the natal chart.

The siang sin star lies to the right of the main number. This is also known as the water star. The number of the siang sin star in the center is the number, which corresponds to the sector where the main door is located. In our examples:

- HOUSE A this number is 5. So the center siang sin star is 5
- HOUSE B the siang sin star in the center is 4 because the main door is located in the Southwest, and the number of the Southwest is 4.

The chor sin star lies to the left of the main number. This is also known as the mountain star. The number of the chor sin star in the center is the number directly opposite the location of the main door.

- HOUSE A the chor sin star in the center is 9
- HOUSE B the chor sin star in the center is 1

HOUSE A

Note in this chart of HOUSE A, the **siang sin star** in the center is **5** and this is the main number of the grid where the main door is located, which is the east. Once you have the center number of the siang sin star, it is then possible to fill in the numbers of the siang sin star for all the nine grids of the Lo Shu. In the example here, the numbers of the siang sin are moving in a positive plus mode from 5 to 6 to 7 according to the flight path …see page 35 to refresh your memory of this flight path …

HOUSE B

In this chart of HOUSE B, note the main door is located in the Southwest where the main number is 4. Thus the center number of the siang sin star is 4.

Now note that the other siang sin star numbers also follow the same flight path but instead of flying in a positive mode, it is now flying in a negative minus mode from 4 to 3 to 2 and so forth. Nevertheless note once again the flight path of the numbers…

CHAPTER
TWO

Flying Star
FENG
SHUI

The
Chor Sin
stars

Flying Star FENG SHUI

HOUSE A

In **HOUSE A** here, the chor sin star in the center is determined to be the number that is the main number of the location directly opposite where the door is.

This is the number 9 which is in the West grid and west is directly opposite East. The rst of the chor sin stars also fly according to the flight path. In this example here note the flight is in positive plus mode, from 9 to 1 to 2 to 3.

HOUSE B

In **HOUSE B** here, note that the center chor sin star is the number that corresponds to the main number of the direction that is opposite where the main door is located. In this example the number is 1 which is in the NE, directly opposite the SW.

Then the rest of the chor sin stars in the other grids of this Lo Shu moves in a positive mode from 1 to 2 to 3 using once again the same flight path. Determining whether stars should fly **positive** or **negative** mode is the next step.

The chor sin star *(also known as the **mountain star**)*

The chor sin star is said to govern the health prospects of the house, and its significance is based on its numeral in the various sector locations in the flying star natal chart of any house. The number that is assigned to each of the chor sin stars in the different sectors indicates the quality of the resident's health during any period of time. Thus when the stars (or numbers) that have flown into the sector where your bedroom is located is afflicted, then your health will definitely take a turn for the worse. Afflicted stars are said to be those with the numbers 5 or 2. These are the numbers that indicate sickness and severe ill health, which can be fatal during any month and year where the flying star numbers of 5 or 2 also happen to fly into the sector.

An auspicious chor sin star is the one that correspond to the number of the period under review. Thus in the period of 7, the chor sin star that is numbered 7 is auspicious - and we must find out where it is located. In our examples please note that:

In HOUSE A the 7 chor sin star is located in the EAST where the main door is also located. This is an auspicious indication for this house. Hence if the residents enhance the chor sin with a mountainous feature (because the chor sin is a mountain star) the good fortune will get magnified. Here the location is East where the element is wood. The 7 star is of the element of metal. Thus energizing wood is of no benefit. Building a wall of brick in the vicinity of the door will be great since wall is of the earth element, which suggests mountain. This is auspicious because the chor sin star must be put up on the "mountain" and not dropped into the "water". This means that there should not be a pond in that particular sector during that particular period of time and instead there should be a wall or a solid object in that sector to symbolize the mountain.

In HOUSE B, the 7 chor sin star is in the Southwest and this is also where the door is located. Once again this is an auspicious orientation for this house during this period of 7. This sector is the Southwest where the element is earth, and is excellent for the mountain star. Thus people living in such a house will generally enjoy good health.

CHAPTER
TWO

Flying Star
FENG
SHUI

The
Siang Sin

Flying Star FENG SHUI

TWO

The siang sin star *(also known as the **water star**)*

The *siang sin star* symbolizes wealth and prosperity prospects. It is also known as the water star, and since is said to be symbolic of riches, having an auspicious water star in the sector where your front door, your office or study is located is said to bring you the luck of wealth and prosperity. Thus If the main door is located where the number 7 siang sin star is found during the period of 7, it is a very auspicious sign for all the residents of the household in that period. Such an auspicious siang sin star is said to be hugely magnified if the door is located to face an open area. Residents will definitely become extremely wealthy during the period of 7. Luck is further improved when some form of water like a fishpond or a fountain, is placed in that sector

In our examples:

HOUSE A has a 3 water star in the sector where the main door is located. The main star numeral is 5. This combination of 3 and 5 is said to cause problems related to sickness and human relationship problems. However the siang sin and chor sin stars add up to 10. DSuch a feature is said to be good. In addition since the East which is the sector where the door is located is of the wood element a 3 water star which is of the same wood element is said to be auspicious.

HOUSE B has a double 7 in the sector of its main door. This is an extremely auspicious feature since a double 7 brings the luck of both the siang sin and chor sin stars during this period of 7. The good fortune will last for 20 years from 1984 to 2003.

The 7 siang sin star is of the metal element and coming into the Southwest, it symbolizes the discovery of *gold in the mountain*. This is because the SW is symbolic of big earth which is the mountain. In addition since the chor sin or mountain star is also 7, the gold is doubled. Good fortune thus comes to the residents continuously all through this twenty year period. In this period it is therefore excellent to have a house that is located in the Southwest, or at least facing the southwest. This statement applies equally in the northern or Southern hemisphere.

STEP FIVE:

The next step is to determine how the chor sin and siang sin secondary stars move. This allows us to complete the natal chart by filling in the numbers of these stars in each of the eight compass sectors of the Lo Shu grid surrounding the center. This part of the computation is a little tricky but if you follow instructions slowly you will soon get the hang of it. To do this you must determine exactly where your main door is located. Reproduced on this page is a simplified feng shui compass which shows that each of the eight sectors is further subdivided into three subsections. You must determine which of these 24 subsections house your main door is located. Be very accurate when taking directions and making measurements.

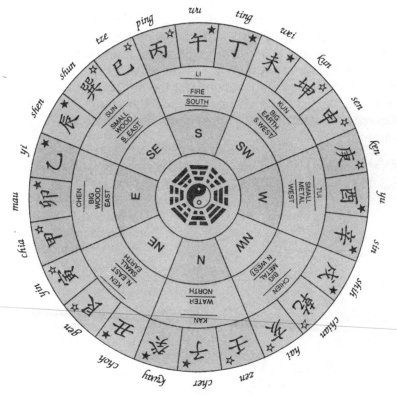

A simplified version of the feng shui compass which shows the three subsectors of each of the eight directions or sectors.

CHAPTER
TWO

Flying Star
FENG
SHUI

Flight of
the
siang sin

Flying Star FENG SHUI

TWO

STEP SIX:
The siang sin and chor sin stars move according to the sector number and exact location of the main door. This movement of the stars can be minus (-) i.e. in the reverse order from say 9 to 8 to 7 to 6 to 5 ... and so on. Or it can be plus (+) i.e. in the normal order, from 1 to 2 to 3 to 4 ... and so on. To determine whether the movement is minus or plus, the computation is similar for both the siang sin star and the chor sin star. **We first look at how the *siang sin star* moves.** We have seen that each of the eight sectors of the compass has three subsections. The movement of the siang sin numbers depends on whether the number of the direction is odd or even and this is different for each of the three subsections. ions.

FOR DOORS LOCATED IN THE CARDINAL DIRECTIONS:
Based on the <u>**original Lo-Shu**</u>, the numbers of the four cardinal directions is odd; South is 9; North is 1; East is 3; and West is 7. For all ODD numbers, the movement is + - - ie. Plus minus minus. This means + for the first subsection, - for the second subsection and - for the third subsection. The subsections of the cardinal directions and their respective plus/minus (+/-) movements are summarized in the diagram here.

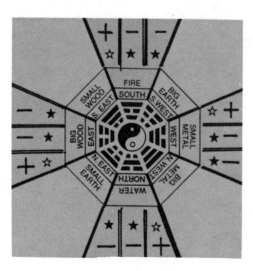

So for the **siang sin** star:

- if your main door is in the first subsection, its movements around the Lo-Shu grid is plus, i.e. normal.

- If it is in the second or third subsections, its movement will be minus (i.e. in reverse direction).

DOORS LOCATED IN THE SECONDARY DIRECTIONS:

Again based on the original Lo-Shu, we note that the numbers of the four secondary directions is EVEN. Thus Southeast is 4; Southwest is 2; Northeast is 8; and Northwest is 6. For all **even** numbers the movement is minus plus plus (i.e. - + +). This means - (minus) when the main door is in the first subsection, and + (plus) when it is in the second or third subsection. Accordingly the siang sin star's movement is minus or plus depending on which subsection the main door is located. Again this is illustrated in the diagram on this page.

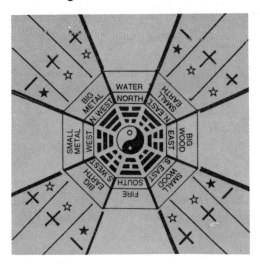

So for the siang sin star located in the secondary directions:

- If the door is in the first subsection its movement around the Lo Shu square is minus ie in the reverse direction.

- If the door is in the second or third subsections the movement is plus ie normal.

STEP SEVEN:
Next it is necessary to determine how the chor sin star moves i.e. whether in a minus (reverse) direction, or in a plus (normal direction).

To determine this, it is first necessary to see what the number of the chor sin star in the center grid is. Look again at the examples of HOUSE A and HOUSE B. Refer to the charts given on page 38 and you will see that the center number chor sin for HOUSE A is 9 and the center number chor sin for HOUSE B is 1. You should also refresh your memory on how this center numebr chor sin was determined.

CHAPTER
TWO

Flying Star
FENG
SHUI

Flight of
the
Chor sin

Flying Star FENG SHUI

The movement of the chor sin star numerals around the Lo Shu grid is based on whether its center number is ODD or EVEN;

If the number is Odd, the flying sequence is + - - ie plus minus minus.
If it is Even, the sequence is - + + ie minus plus plus.

Thus in our example **HOUSE A:** the chor sin number in the center is 9, which is Odd. Because we have determined that the main door is located in the first subsection of the direction East, the movement of the HOUSE A's chor sin star is plus. Thus note the chor sin moves from 9 to 1 to 2 and so on.

In **HOUSE B** the center number of the chor sin star is also odd, i.e. the number 1, and because the main door of the house B was also deemed to be in the first subsection, the movement of its chor sin star around the grid is also plus; (again following the sequence + - - ie. plus minus minus.

APPLYING THE ABOVE FORMULA:

Once you have mastered the flying star formula and have developed a working facility with the drawing up the Lo-Shu time chart (or natal chart) on paper, You will be in a position to use the formula on your house or office. Start by superimposing the Lo-Shu square onto your house or office plan. Make sure these plans are drawn to scale and are accurate.

The essence of the Lo-Shu is the implied balance of space divisions! Obviously it is impossible to exactly "fit" the square onto the average house or office plan. To get round this problem, feng shui masters make very exact measurements of the house being studied or investigated so that the division of the house into nine equal grids is as accurate as possible. They do not need to be square but they do need to be equal in size. This ensures that the division into sectors (grids) according to directions is accurate since so much of feng shui practical applications is based on directional accuracy.

Having said this however, some feng shui Masters' way of interpreting the luck of the respective sectors of the house do not depend so much on this. Instead they place more emphasis on the actual design of the layout. Thus for houses that are long and deep with only one room that takes up the whole width of the house, analysis is based only on the center vertical panel of the Lo Shu square's numbers.

When the house being investigated has two rooms in the width then analysis is based on the two outer vertical panels of numbers. This aspect of the analysis will be dealt with in greater detail later.

In the meanwhile for those of you readers who simply cannot master the computation of the natal chart of houses, in the following pages, I have worked out the sixteen different natal charts of all houses belonging to the period of 7.

Those of you who do know how to compute the Lo Shu natal chart will find that you are able to apply the formula to houses of any period.

Chapter Three
Natal Charts for period 7 houses

FLYING STAR FACING DIRECTIONS OF THE MAIN DOOR

FACING DIRECTION	WHEN BEARING DEGREES
SOUTH 1	157.5 to 172.5
SOUTH 2	172.5 to 187.5
SOUTH 3	187.5 to 202.5
SOUTHWEST 1	202.5 to 217.5
SOUTHWEST 2	217.5 to 232.5
SOUTHWEST 3	232.5 to 247.5
WEST 1	247.5 to 262.5
WEST 2	262.5 to 277.5
WEST 3	277.5 to 292.5
NORTHWEST 1	292.5 to 307.5
NORTHWEST 2	307.5 to 322.5
NORTHWEST 3	322.5 to 337.5
NORTH 1	337.5 to 352.5
NORTH 2	352.5 to 007.5
NORTH 3	007.5 to 022.5
NORTHEAST 1	022.5 to 037.5
NORTHEAST 2	037.5 to 052.5
NORTHEAST 3	052.5 to 067.5
EAST 1	067.5 to 082.5
EAST 2	082.5 to 097.5
EAST 3	097.5 to 112.5
SOUTHEAST 1	112.5 to 127.5
SOUTHEAST 2	127.5 to 142.5
SOUTHEAST 3	142.5 to 157.5

HOUSES WITH DOORS
IN FIRST SUBSECTION OF THE NORTH SECTOR.

SE	S	SW
3 2 6 7	7 2 2 5	5 4 4 9
4 1 5	2- 3+ 7	9 5 9
8 6 1	6 8 3	1 4 8
NE	N	NW

Right: The Star numbers have been turned to aid in analysis. So NORTH is shown in the top grid.

1 8 4	6 3 8 N	8 1 6
9 9 5	2 7 3	4 5 1
5 4 9	7 2 7 S	3 6 2

The house has an <u>auspicious front door</u> with the 8-water star and the 6-mountain star. Placing water flowing towards the house's front door will bring great and enormous prosperity. * The <u>back door is also prosperous</u>. Thus for period 7 having a door <u>placed north</u> and <u>facing the first subsection of North</u> is very auspicious. * The <u>quarrelsome sectors</u> are the center of the house and the Southeast. Husbands and wives will quarrel a lot if the master bedroom is placed in these sectors. This is due to the 3/2 combination. The 2/3 of the center is known as *stubborn fighting killing sha. This cause disputes, arguments, lawsuits, complaints, back stabbing and intense hostility from outsiders to befall the residents. Overcome this with small amounts of metal and fire elements (ie red & gold). Keep the place of the 3/2 very quiet !* The 3/2 of the SE cause disputes in business leading to loss and lawsuits. Remedy with fire element. * The <u>NE and South sectors</u> of this house are very lucky. Put important rooms in these parts of the house. In the NE is the wonderfully lucky combination of 8/6 which indicates wealth and power. If your bedroom is located here in this sector you will enjoy wealth luck. Enhance with earth energy * South has <u>the auspicious double 7</u> very lucky in the period of 7 but in period of 8 leads to armed robbery ! * The <u>4/1 combination in the NW and in the East</u> spells romance/love luck and scholarly achievements. BUT excessive water in either sector causes sex scandals. Balance is vital. Grow water lilies and lotus to attract the good without the bad. * The 5/9 and 9/5 combinations in the West and SW are very dangerous. In very rare situations this combination brings great wealth luck but often it merely causes severe mental and financial afflictions. Pressure and stress usually result. Use metal to combat.

CHAPTER
THREE

Natal
Chart for
period 7
houses

North 2/3

Natal Charts for period 7 houses | **Three**

**HOUSES WITH DOORS IN THE
SECOND & THIRD SUBSECTION OF THE NORTH SECTOR.**

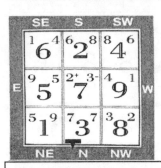

Right: the star numerals
have been turned to place
North on top to facilitate
ease of analysis

$3 8_2$	$7 3_7$	$5 1_9$
$4 9_1$	$2 7_3$	$9 5_5$
$8 4_6$	$6 2_8$	$1 6_4$

This house has a very **auspicious front door** with the double 7. This means both the water star and the mountain star are auspicious during this period of 7. If you build a water feature in full view of the door, the luck of prosperity will benefit all residents within the home. * The **back door is equally auspicious** with a 6 mountain star. Thus if you build a wall behind to support the door, it will be another strong lucky feature. Since the back is South and of the fire element, tapping the mountain star is an excellent and fast way to prosperity. * The main obstacle indicated by the flying star chart for this house is the **severe affliction indicated for family harmony** (the center) and **for the patriarch** (the Northwest). Note both locations have the quarrelsome 3/2 combination of small numbers. This means there will be plenty of shouting, anger, arguments and disharmony amongst residents in the house. But there is also a great deal of money, which hopefully should offer some consolation. * Do not have a bedroom in the East and NE grids. The occurrence of two number 5's in the East will cause anyone staying in this sector to succumb to severe illness. Also, the 5/9 combinations in both grids spell severe problems related to health and money. Use metal to exhaust the earth 5 or water to overcome it might be helpful. Different masters recommend different solutions and remedies to counter the 5/9 * The 1/4 combination in the SE will cause there to be romance luck associated with money but if there is a water feature in this corner, romance is of a scandalous nature (e.g. where one or both parties are already married indulging in an illicit union.) The 4/1 combination in the West tends to bring romance of the safer kind. Again there is money in the love luck. Enhance with metal, but do not use windchimes. Let it be quiet metal otherwise the romance turns scandalous *

HOUSES WITH DOORS IN THE
FIRST SUBSECTION OF THE SOUTH SECTOR.

S ↑

SE	S	SW
2 6 3	7 2 7	9 4 5
1 5 4	3^+ 7 2	5 9 9
6 1 8	8 3 6	4 8 1

E ... W
NE N NW

Right: No need to turn the grid since South is already on top.

2 6 3	7 2 7	9 4 5
1 5 4	3 7 2	5 9 9
6 1 8	8 3 6	4 8 1

* This house has the **excellent double 7 stars** in the grid where the **front door** is located. It is unfortunate that the main star numeral is 2 causing some hiccups and obstacles but generally the door is good. Place a plant near the front door to press down on the inauspicious 2. * **The WEST sector is seriously bad**. The 5/9 combination create severe stress and problems for anyone sleeping or working in this sector. Hang a curved knife here to counter this inauspicious star combination. The best room in the house is the room in the NE sector where the combination of 1, 6 and 8 stars bring enormous good fortune to anyone staying there. These are the three "white stars" and are considered highly prized in flying star feng shui analysis. Thus the Patriarch should hopefully occupy this sector – it should house the master bedroom. You should make sure the toilet or kitchen is not placed in this part of the house. * Meanwhile the NW is the sector with the romance luck, and the main numeral being 8 brings money with love. * In the SW the water star is 5 so place a plant here to dissolve the effect of this 5, and if this proves insufficient to overcome the 5/9 combination, use metal as well to exhaust the strengthened 5 earth energy. A young but very intelligent feng shui practitioner friend of mine uses a very novel method - he recommends hanging a *metal mountain* here to counter the bad stars. He says he has used this remedy with considerable success. His metal mountain is a copper tooling piece of artwork ! * In the **west** the mountain star is 5 so place a bright light here to counter this unlucky but strengthened star numeral. * Avoid having a family room in the center because of the 3/2 combination. This causes disharmony amongst siblings and between parents.

CHAPTER
THREE

Natal
Chart for
period 7
houses

South 2/3

Natal Charts for period 7 houses

Three

HOUSES WITH DOORS IN THE
SECOND & THIRD SUBSECTION OF THE SOUTH SECTOR.

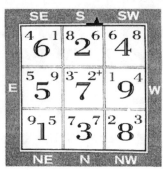

4**6**1	8**2**6	6**4**8
5**5**9	3**7**2	1**9**4
9**1**5	7**3**7	2**8**3

Right: There was no need to turn the Grid since South is already on top.

* This house has good stars in the grid which houses the **front door** with the 6 water star and the 8 mountain star. However because the direction is south whose element is fire, placing a water feature here could well cause the elements to clash. A water feature is therefore not recommended in the vicinity of the front door in spite of the lucky 6 star. It would also afflict the lucky mountain star, which has the 8 numeral causing the mountain to fall into the water. An excellent solution is to enhance the earth energy here with crystals. This makes the door even more auspicious. * There are two 5 numerals in the East grid and this indicates a severely afflicted East sector. Do not place anyone in any bedroom in this sector during this period of 7 since the double 5 will cause the ripening of illness karma. Children staying in this sector could succumb to frequent illness. **Place a 5 rod windchime or hang a curved knife to exhaust the double 5 of the East grid**. Note also that the sector combination is 5/9 which is itself a severely bad combination. A windchime with a pagoda top is the answer to the problem here. * The Northwest and the center are negatively affected by the 3/2 combination. Keep these two places as quiet as possible. No noise, otherwise quarrels and arguments could well become violent. The 3/2 combination always cause disharmony in relationships. I have discovered that placing some quiet water here does succeed in soothing ruffled feathers. Try it ! * The luckiest grid in the house is the North (the back area) with the double 7 and the Southwest 6/8. Energize these two sectors and place all your important rooms here. Make sure not to have your kitchen, maids room or store room in either of these two sectors.

HOUSES WITH DOORS IN THE
FIRST SUBSECTION OF THE EAST SECTOR.

SE $8^{\,4}6$	S $4^{\,9}2$	SW $6^{\,2}4$
E $7^{\,3}5$	$9^{+\,5^{+}}7$	$2^{\,7}9$ W
$3^{\,8}1$	$5^{\,1}3$	$1^{\,6}8$
NE	N	NW

Right: the star numerals are turned to bring **east** to the top for easy analysis

	E	
$3\,1\,8$	$7\,5\,3$	$8\,6\,4$
N $5\,3\,1$	$9\,7\,5$	$4\,2\,9$ S
$1\,8\,6$	W $2\,9\,7$	$6\,4\,2$

- * In this house the main door is facing the first subsection of East direction and is also located in the east where the main star numeral is 5. Generally for this period of 7, a **main door in the East does not bring any luck.** The door should also not be moved to either the NE or the SE since the number combinations of both grids are considered very harmful to the children of the family. * In the above house chart the water and mountains star numerals of the main door grid add up to 10 and this brings some good news. There will be some months when the luck brought in by the front door is excellent but luck is not consistent. * The **luckiest sector is the northwest** where the three numbers 1, 6 and 8 bring exceptional good luck to anyone staying in that corner of the house. If the master bedroom is located here the Patriarch benefits enormously. He will likely be very shrewd financially and his good fortune at the share market extends to the whole family. **Place a wealth vase** filled with semi precious stones in this corner to energize and magnify the good fortune of this corner for the breadwinner. * The other **sectors SE and the NE** grids have luck but are harmful to the children. If a water feature with a sole **tortoise is placed in the North** sector this will activate the auspicious water star of the North bringing money and success to the house. * The 5/1 combination in the North will cause anyone having a bedroom here to have problems related to hearing disabilities and sex diseases. A metal ornament can counter this.

CHAPTER
THREE

Natal
Chart for
period 7
houses

East 2/3

Natal Charts for period 7 houses

Three

HOUSES WITH DOORS IN THE
SECOND & THIRD SUBSECTION OF THE EAST SECTOR.

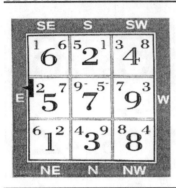

Right: The star numerals are turned to bring East to the top for easy analysis.

6 **1** 2	2 **5** 7	1 **6** 6
4 **3** 9	9 **7** 5	5 **2** 1
8 **8** 4	7 **9** 3	3 **4** 8

* In this house the main door is also located in the east where the main star numeral 5 cause problems during this period of 7. However the water star of the main door in this house is the auspicious 7 so **a water feature placed here in the East** would be lucky for the house. Build a small waterfall where the water is flowing towards the house (not away from the house). This also serves the purpose of dealing with the unlucky mountain star 2. Letting it "fall into the water" is an excellent remedy. * The lucky sectors of this house are the **SW and the NE.** In both these sectors the water stars are auspicious because they are of the earth element flying into earth sectors. Thus **in the SW the star numeral 8 enhances** the auspicious essence of grid. If the matriarch of the house stays here it is exceptionally lucky for her. In the NE the earth element numeral 2 also enhances this sector's element and with the numeral 6 mountain star it signifies *gold found in the mountain*. Also the main numeral of this grid is 1 which is also a lucky number. **This makes the NE extremely lucky**. It is a good idea to energize the sector with a "pretend" mountain of gold. Simulate this by creating a small mound in the garden made up of stones that have been painted a gold colour. It will bring prosperity luck. Or hang a copper mountain painting here. * The combination of 1/6 in the SE sector indicates residents have great financial skills and high intelligence. During months when 5 visits however, there is risk of excessive mental pressure. The South sector with the 5 mountain star in a main star 2 is bad. And the center with the 5/9 combination is also bad. Family suffers from illness and disharmony. Use a windchime to press down the bad luck.

HOUSES WITH DOORS IN THE
FIRST SUBSECTION OF THE WEST SECTOR.

W ↑

SE	S	SW
$4\,^8 6$	$9\,^4 2$	$2\,^6 4$
$3\,^7 5$	$5^+\,^{9+} 7$	$7\,^2 9$
$8\,^3 1$	$1\,^5 3$	$6\,^1 8$

E ◄ ... ► W

NE   N   NW

Right: West has been placed on top to facilitate analysis, so the numbers have also moved.

$2\,4\,6$	$7\,9\,2$	$6\,8\,1$
S $9\,2\,4$	$5\,7\,9$	$1\,3\,5$ **N**
$4\,6\,8$	$3\,5\,7$	$8\,1\,3$

* In this house the <u>water star</u> of the main door's sector is the unlucky number 2. However because this sector is west, and because 2 represents the earth element, it is beneficial. This is because the earth produces metal. The **main door is therefore not afflicted by the 2**. The mountain star is the lucky **7** so the main door is lucky. But the 2/7 combination brings bad luck for children; they are better off living away from home. An excellent idea with this house is to have the door moved to the NW grid to capture the excellent luck of the 6/1 combination. Moving the door to the other corner ie to the SW (still facing west) is also good. Here the 2/6 combination brings an affluent lifestyle with little stress. This is further enhanced by hanging a windchime. . * The sector **NW is especially auspicious**. This is the sector of the breadwinner and the 1/6 combination indicates he has superb financial luck. The water star in this sector is 1 which is auspicious. It means prosperity luck has arrived. So it **is vital to energize the water star with a 6 rod windchime** here. Remember metal produces water. That the mountain star is the numeral 6 compounds and enhances the luck. On no account should this sector be destroyed by having a toilet or kitchen here. If you do it is a tremendous waste of good feng shui since this is the luckiest part of the house. * At the back of the house in the east sector with the afflicted 3/7 combination sitting on a 5 main star numeral. * The East is especially bad and anyone with a bedroom in this sector will get robbed and mugged. There could even be violence so move out of there ! This situation is not so bad during period 7 but when 8 period comes it is a major problem. Place a water feature here to counter the bad stars combination. Let the water be reasonably close.

CHAPTER
THREE

Natal
Chart for
period 7
houses

West 2/3

Natal Charts for period 7 houses

Three

HOUSES WITH DOORS IN THE
SECOND & THIRD SUBSECTION OF THE WEST SECTOR.

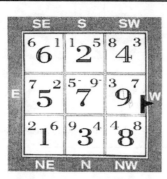

8**4**3	3**9**7 (W)	4**8**8
1**2**5 (S)	5**7**9	9**3**4 (N)
6**6**1	7**5**2 (E)	2**1**6

Right: West has been placed on top and the star numbers moved to aid analysis.

* In this house the water star of the main door's sector is the **lucky number 7** and it also adds up to 10 when combined with the 3 mountain star. This is an auspicious manifestation of flying star. Hang a 7 rod windchime near the front door to activate this lucky water star. But please note that the **3/7** combination indicates armed robbery. This is definite to happen in the period of 8 but can also happen in the present period. Residents should thus be security conscious. * The **back door sector in the East is seriously afflicted.** Here the water star is 2 and the main star numeral is 5. The numbers 2 and 5 occurring together cause severe danger to the health of anyone staying in that sector or for the residents if a public area like the dining or family room is placed here. The 2/7 combination also brings bad luck to children. And the 5 main numeral suggest danger related to fire. Also during some months of the year when the 2 or 5 is the **lo shu** of that month the danger becomes acute. It is a good idea not to have the back door located in that sector. Move it to the NE or SE. It is also a good idea to place the kitchen or the store room in the East since this contains the bad stars effectively. * The sector **South is also dangerous**. Once again we see the two unlucky numerals of 2 and 5 occurring together. The water star is afflicted and this being the sector of fire, anyone staying here could succumb to a fatal illness related to kidneys or sex organs, or suffer financial and family loss. Place a large windchime here to suppress the bad energy or locate a toilet or store room here to contain the bad energy. Some Masters suggest using metal to exhaust the strong but afflicted earth energy. Still others recommend water. Personally I have always found windchimes to be an excellent deterrent for the bad stars 5 and 2.

HOUSES WITH DOORS IN THE FIRST SUBSECTION OF THE SOUTHWEST SECTOR.

Right: the SW has been placed on top for ease of analysis.

$5\mathbf{2}_9$	SW $7\mathbf{4}_7$	W $3\mathbf{9}_2$
SE $9\mathbf{6}_5$	$1\mathbf{7}_4$	NW $2\mathbf{8}_3$
$8\mathbf{5}_6$	NE $4\mathbf{1}_1$	$6\mathbf{3}_8$

* This house enjoys a very auspicious front door where it benefits enormously from the double 7 water and mountain stars. The 7 is generally lucky for this period up to 2003. But those with this situation must remember that come period of 8 all the good luck gets transformed into bad luck and the double 7 then cause armed robbery to occur- usually with some violence involved. So the door needs to be changed <u>before</u> the period of 8. For now, this **SW corner benefits the earth mother**. Thus in this house it is the women and especially the matriarch who benefits most from the auspicious feng shui. Anything undertaken by the matriarch is sure to succeed. To ensure this luck is sustained throughout the whole period, keep the SW well lighted. * This house suffers from **two quarrelsome grids – the West and the NW** both with the horrible 3/2 combination. The father, or man of the family will be quarrelsome, and children tend to be argumentative. This is because the **NW and the West are afflicted**. Placing water features – ponds and aquariums here should calm ruffled feathers. Or place fire with metal (red and gold) here to control the bad stars. Those sleeping in these sectors should ensure their bedrooms stay very quiet. * **The North grid is auspicious**. It enjoys the mountain 6 star and water 8 star. The 6/8 combination brings wealth and popularity, power and authority, and these goodies can be enhanced with earth or water elements. * **The Northeast is also lucky** as it brings popularity and love to residents. It should house the family or dining room. Plants here and a small water feature is excellent but too much water could lead to sex scandals. **The South and Southeast are seriously afflicted.** The 5/9 combinations here cause stress and mental afflictions. Use metal to overcome but let it be quiet metal.

CHAPTER
THREE

Natal
Chart for
period 7
houses

Southwest
2/3

Natal Charts for period 7 houses

Three

**HOUSES WITH DOORS IN THE SECOND/THIRD SUBSECTION
OF THE SOUTHWEST SECTOR.**

Right: the SW grid is on top
for ease of analysis

SW		
6 **2** 8	4 **4** 1	8 **9** 6
2 **6** 3	1 **7** 4	9 **8** 5
E **5** 2	NE **1** 7	N **3** 9
3	7	5

* This house enjoys a lucky water star in the front door . The number 1 itself is of the water element so there is no need to build a water feature here to enhance the luck. The presence of the number 4 however indicates an excess of wood element, which in the SW is not a good feature. This is because wood exhausts and destroys earth, and earth is very important to the SW unless it becomes afflicted. In this case it has not. The solution is to place a small metal curved knife in this sector to control the wood. A metal windchime is also a good idea. Meanwhile note that the 4/1 combination, while it brings romance and social popularity luck can also lead to scandals when there is an excess of water. * The back door area of this **house enjoys the double 7**. If the back door is located in the NE therefore, the house will enjoy excellent feng shui. But make sure that the kitchen is not also placed here since this could press down on the good luck of the two 7s. Upstairs this sector would be ideal as a family area so that everyone benefits from the good feng shui. * The most **unlucky room in this house is the EAST**... it is very severely bad. This is because all three star numerals indicate fatal illness, extreme loss and even death. The **5 and 2 together is extremely unlucky**, and with the 3 thrown in, the whole effect is one of destruction and tears. The combination of 3/2 is also regarded as most inauspicious and for those in business it leads to law suits. Everything is most disharmonious. Place a toilet in this grid area to flush away all the bad luck. Some feng shui masters recommend that placing red and gold paper here to simulate fire and metal (perhaps in wallpaper) is an effective way to control the 3/2. *

HOUSES WITH DOORS IN THE FIRST SUBSECTION OF THE SOUTHEAST SECTOR.

SE	S	SW
$9\,6\,7$	$4\,2\,2$	$2\,4\,9$
E $1\,5\,8$	8^-6^- 7	$6\,4$ 9 W
$5\,1\,3$	$3\,3\,1$	$7\,8\,5$
NE	N	NW

Right: The grid has been turned around to place SE on top. This aids analysis.

SE		
$1\mathbf{5}8$	$9\mathbf{6}7$	$4\mathbf{2}2$
NE $5\mathbf{1}3$	$8\mathbf{7}6$	SW $2\mathbf{4}9$
$3\mathbf{3}1$	$7\mathbf{8}5$ NW	$6\mathbf{9}4$

* This house enjoys moderate luck. The **front door in the SE has a lucky water star** 7 numeral. But 7 is of the metal element and coming into the corner of wood (the SE is of the wood element) cause the energies to be in disharmony. Thus any good luck experienced is soon dissipated and is therefore temporary. The 7/9 combination suggests fire hazards and huge problems caused by over indulgence in sex and flirtations. It is a good idea to use water or earth element objects to control the afflicted stars. There is also an **unhealthy SOUTH** grid where the double 2 numerals create the bad luck of loss and illness,. The 4/2 combination can also cause problems with in laws and illnesses associated with the internal organs. Again use water to overcome this affliction. Do not have a bedroom in the south part of the home. **The NW, which is traditionally the place of the Patriarch, has an afflicted water star**. The 5 star numeral here cause the water star to bring illness to this grid. The 5/7 combination indicates problems associated with the mouth and this means either mouth related diseases OR danger of poisoning OR problems caused by excessive chatter. Use water to overcome this affliction. The **north sector** has an excellent 3/1 combination which suggests wealth and popularity but this sector will also benefit from the presence of water. This is because the north is of the water element. To have a lucky water star here and with the number 1 being water as well, good fortune comes easily. Do not overdo things however and stay balanced. The NE with the 5/3 combination is extremely bad for wealth. It is worse here because the 5 is the mountain star. Do not have your bedroom here and do not energize anything here.

CHAPTER
THREE

Natal
Chart for
period 7
houses

Southeast
2/3

Natal Charts for period 7 houses | Three

HOUSES WITH DOORS IN THE SECOND & THIRD SUBSECTION OF THE SOUTHEAST SECTOR.

SE	S	SW
⁷6⁵	³2¹	⁵4³
⁶5⁴	⁸⁺7⁶⁺	¹9⁸
²1⁹	⁴3²	⁹8⁷
NE	N	NW

SE		
6**5**4	7**6**5	3**2**1
NE 2**1**9	8**7**6	SW 5**4**3
4**3**2	NW 9**8**7	1**9**8

Right: The SE grid has been moved to the top for ease of analysis.

* This house has an **afflicted water star numeral 5** in the front door grid ie in the SE. The whole family and indeed, all the residents will suffer from this afflicted flying star. It is a good idea to try and find another door as this is a seriously bad feature that brings bad luck to the house. The combination of 5/7 indicate gossip and bad reputation. It also causes illness relating to the mount. The bad luck is experienced in both periods 7 and 8. Placing a large green plant near the front door will dissolve the bad luck but not completely. Some Masters recommend using water, while others suggest metal (like a windchime) to overcome the bad stars, but in my opinion water will be a bad solution and metal does not help. The best solution is to move the door. Moving to the South brings wealth luck but could cause residents to have to move out ! Moving to the E has the 5 center numeral and the 4/6 combination will be abd for the women of the household. * This house is weighed under by the **3/2 quarrelsome stars in the South, and in the North**. But the 3/1 combination in the South suggests wealth and popularity while the 4/2 of the North indicates health problems related to malfunctioning of the internal organs. The best way to counter this affliction in the North is to place an urn filled with water here. This cools down fiery tempers and overcomes health problems to some extent. In the South activate the wealth aspects of the good combination stars with water. This energizes the auspicious 1 water star while simultaneously calming tempers caused by the 3.2 quarrelsome stars. The 4/6 of the East indicates bad luck for the women of the household who will suffer indignities. There is no specific cure. Women should not sleep here. The 2/9 of the NE indicates sluggishness and simple mindedness. Not good for College children as this hurts their grades.

HOUSES WITH DOORS IN THE FIRST SUBSECTION OF THE NORTHEAST SECTOR.

Grid (left):

SE	S	SW
5 9 6	9 5 2	7 7 4
6 8 5	4 1 7	2 3 9
1 4 1	8 6 3	3 2 8

E ... W

NE | N | NW

Right: the Grid has been turned to place NE on top

Main chart:

	NE	
8 3 6	1 1 4	6 5 8
NW 3 8 2	4 7 1	SE 5 6 9
2 9 3	SW 7 4 7	9 2 5

* This house has **the 1/4 combination in the NE where the main door is located**. This indicates scholarly achievements, media attention, publicity and romance The water star 4 represents wood in the mountain. This is not good. The mountain star 1 strengthens the earth element of the NE thereby bringing good luck. The main door is not afflicted. * The **back door in the SW has the auspicious double 7** combination of water and mountain stars indicating luck coming when least expected - like gold being discovered in the mountain - a good sign. The double 7 is lucky only in the period of 7. When the Time Cycle changes to the 8 period it becomes dangerous and indicates armed robbery. So either change the natal chart altogether or remedy the situation after 2003 by pressing down the 7s with fire element. This means bright lights kept turned on through the night. * **The Southeast and South sectors are afflicted with the 5/9 and 9/5** combinations. These are bad luck, stress, pressure and illness stars. Overcoming these combinations do not draw a consensus amongst Master practitioners of flying star feng shui. Some suggest using sturdy plants to control the earth of 5 while enhancing the fire of 9. Others suggest metal to exhaust the earth of 5 and aggravate the fire of 9. I advise not to sleep in these two sectors if possible, and to place a store room here. **The NW and West have the quarrelsome 2/3 and 3/2 combinations**. Using red and gold will help to alleviate the bad chi of these sectors. The North and the East benefit from the 6/8 and 8/6 combinations which bring wealth and prosperity. But the East has the main numeral 5 which cause obstacles to wealth and the North has the main star numeral of 3 which is also not auspicious. To enjoy good luck therefore, strengthen the water and mountain stars with element enhancers to get the best of the good combinations

CHAPTER
THREE

Natal
Chart for
period 7
houses

Northeast
2/3

Natal Charts for period 7 houses | Three

HOUSES WITH DOORS IN THE SECOND & THIRD SUBSECTION OF THE NORTHEAST SECTOR.

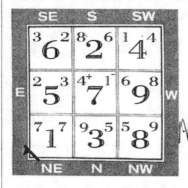

Right: The NE has been moved to the top to aid analysis.

This house has **the auspicious double 7** combination of water and mountain stars in the **NE where the main door is located** - an excellent combination that spells excellent wealth and success luck for this period of 7. When the Time Cycle changes to 8 it indicates armed robbery. Thus the door has to be changed before the 2003 when period of 8 starts. When considering this please remember to check the renovation taboos connected with the Grand Duke and so forth. * The **back door in the SW has** the 1/4 combination. This is excellent and should be enhanced with a high wall at the back to tap the auspicious mountain star. The 1/4 combination also indicates romance coming by the back door ! * **The Nortwhest and North sectors are afflicted with the 5/9 and 9/5** combinations. These are bad luck, stress, pressure and illness stars. Different masters offer different remedies for overcoming these combinations. Hong Kong masters suggest using wood element to control the 5 earth while enhancing the 9 fire. Other Practitioners use metal to exhaust the 5 earth and aggravate the 9 fire. Still others suggest placing a small store room to imprison the bad stars !. * **The SE and East have the quarrelsome 2/3 and 3/2 combinations**. Using red and gold will help to alleviate the bad chi of these sectors. * **The South and the West benefit from the 6/8 and 8/6 combinations** which bring wealth and prosperity. It would thus appear that the back of the house is far more lucky than the front in terms of locations for bedrooms. * **There is also the auspicious 1/4 in the SW** and this brings fame and recognition to the women of the household. But on no account should there be water placed in this sector since water spoils everything and will turn fame into notoriety and recognition into scandal.

HOUSES WITH DOORS IN THE FIRST SUBSECTION OF THE NORTHWEST SECTOR.

SE	S	SW
7^96	$2^{4}2^{}$ ($^2 2^4$)	$9^{}4^2$
$8^{}5^1$	$6^{-}7^{8-}$	$4^{}9^6$
$3^{}1^5$	$1^{}3^3$	$5^{}8^7$

E ... W

NE N NW

Right: the NW has been moved to the top to aid analysis

	NW	
$4\mathbf{9}6$	$5\mathbf{8}7$	$1\mathbf{3}3$
SW $9\mathbf{4}2$	$6\mathbf{7}8$	NE $3\mathbf{1}5$
$2\mathbf{2}4$	SE $7\mathbf{6}9$	$8\mathbf{5}1$

The <u>main door of this house has the lucky 7</u> numeral for the water star and the unlucky 5 numeral for the mountain star. Because this is the NW sector, which has metal as its element, the 7 star enhances this metal and therefore creates good harmony. The 5 star is of the earth element which produces metal. On balance therefore the main door is fine in this period of 7. But the 5/7 combination is a negative one and in the next period residents will suffer from gossip and loss of reputation.

- The South sector suffers from the presence of the double 2 star numerals and with a 2/4 combination which indicate marriage and in-law problems. Best not to have master bedroom here.
- The 2/9 of the SW spells bad luck for children's education luck. Avoid bedrooms for them in this grid.
- The NE has the unlucky 3/5 combination which means loss of wealth and cash flow problems a plenty. Overcome this with passive metal although this will only be partly successful. Best to have a store room here to capture the bad stars. Do not work or sleep here.
- The 4/6 combination in the West grid indicates it is most unsuitable for the daughters of the family. Place sons here instead.
- The center of the house is the most auspicious sector with its 8/6 combination of water and mountain stars. It is a good idea to place the master bedroom in the center of the house.

CHAPTER
THREE

Natal
Chart for
period 7
houses

Northwest
2/3

Natal Charts for period 7 houses | **Three**

HOUSES WITH DOORS IN THE SECOND & THIRD SUBSECTION OF THE NORTHWEST SECTOR.

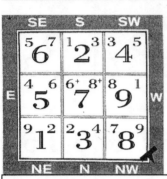

Right: The NW has been moved to the top for easier analysis.

NW		
8 9 1	7 8 9	2 3 4
SW 3 4 5	6 7 8	**NE** 9 1 2
1 2 3	**SE** 5 6 7	4 5 6

The main door of this house has **three lucky numerals**: 9 for the water star , 7 for the mountain star and 8 for the main star numeral. This indicates continued prosperity for the family … present, future and distant prosperity are all indicated. This generally means good fortune for the descendants as well. The good fortune will be better in the next period than in this present period. The 7/9 combination however indicates that the men of the family tend to have roving eyes and have affairs outside the marriage.

- This house suffers from **two bad corners** which are **afflicted by the 2/3** quarrelsome combination. In the north the mountain star 2 combines with the main numeral star 3 to indicate a great deal of arguments and misunderstandings. Place a big urn filled with water to cope with these two stars. The 2/4 combinations indicates severe marriage problems.
- In the south the water star numeral is 3 and this number is of the wood element. This feeds the fire of this sector causing grievous problems and even violence because of the 3/2 combination. In this grid the 3/2 configuration is much more serious than in the North grid. Place a very large presence of water here to cool down the fire. The 1/3 combination which usually means wealth is in this case afflicted. It indicates someone leaving home instead. Water alleviates this problem.
- The NE corner is also afflicted with the 2/9 combination. This brings bad luck for studies and education so here do not energize NE for your College or school going children.

The movement of heaven ...

The movement of Heaven is full of power
The superior man makes himself strong and untiring

From the I CHING on the Trigram CHIEN

Chapter Four
Applications of Flying Star feng shui

Mountains standing close together
The superior man
does not permit his thoughts
To go beyond his situation

From the I CHING on the Trigram KEN

Applications of Flying Star feng shui | **Four**

The method of computation illustrated in the preceding two chapters introduced the concept of the secondary flying stars - the *siang sin stars* and the *chor sin stars*. Based on the Lo-Shu chart drawn up with that method, a great deal of information about the feng shui of the house is revealed. The next stage is to proceed from there to analyze the meanings of all the numerals "assigned" to the stars in each and all of the nine squares of the Lo-Shu.

Usually FENG SHUI Masters adept with flying star will begin by analyzing the luck of the house in the entire twenty period. We have seen that the current 20 year period ends in 2003 and this is the period of 7. After reading the "luck" of the house for this period, we can then proceed to fine tune the applications by then investigating the quality of the time dimension feng shui luck for each year, and even each month. Thus we can use flying star to work out the luck – good as well as bad – over the following twelve months. This is what feng shui masters in Hong Kong are generally engaged to work out. Needless to say, all indications of bad luck are accompanied by advice on what can be done to overcome the bad luck.

Depending on how the secondary star number combine with each other in the nine squares, it is possible to identify auspicious and inauspicious corners of any house of office during this 7 period. In this period the main numeral of the center square is 7. This center number is the key to the placement of the rest of the other numbers in the other grids that make up the Lo-Shu square. As such, the method - with 7 in the center - **also represents the Natal Chart** of all the houses and office buildings built/constructed and completed between the years 1984 to 2003. Thus to investigate if a newly built house will be auspicious for the rest of the period, we simply need to draw up this natal chart to discover the effect of flying star feng shui on the new house.

To simplify matters I have also computed the sixteen natal charts of houses of this period so that readers who find difficulty in making the computation themselves can identify which of the charts is their house and then proceed from there to read on to go deeper into the feng shui of their homes and to make whatever adjustments necessary.
See these charts in Chapter Three on pages 47 to 62

Applications of Flying Star feng shui | Four

Likewise, if you are presently building a new house, it is advisable that in addition to factoring in good directions and orientations, one should also undertake a time dimension analysis using flying star. This procedure gives added depth to the practice of feng shui, thereby making it more "complete".

Meanings are assigned to each of the main star numerals, and to a very large extent, these meanings are associated with their symbolic element representations; as well as how the elements they symbolize interact with the elements originally assigned to each of the directions/sectors.

Lest this sounds too complex, please take heart. Once you study the case examples given, you will start to understand and appreciate the analysis quite easily. All feng shui practice, irrespective of the method used or the school being followed, spring from the same foundation and the origins of the underlying concepts of balance and harmony do not differ. So when you find yourself being stuck by some apparent contradiction or by an analysis which seems strange, just think it through and try to apply the yin/yang balance or the five element theory to the problem at hand. The solution will soon become clear. Use the examples given to walk you through the different factors to consider when making the analysis.

Interpretations and meanings are based on similar symbols. The same symbols govern all the different schools of feng shui Thus the Trigrams of the Pa-Kua, the relationship cycles of the five elements, the forces associated with each of the four cardinal and four secondary directions are similar. Where methods and schools differ are in the methods of computation. And where feng shui masters differ are in the subtleties and nuances of interpretations.

Flying Star Feng Shui addresses the time dimension. The old Masters who developed the method of computation use the ancient Chinese Ganzhi calendar system of heavenly stems and earthly branches to work out relevant reigning numbers for the 20 year periods. Similarly the manuals have also worked out the relevant reigning numbers for each of the different lunar years AND for the different lunar months.

Using these reigning numbers the feng shui practitioner can then use the Flying Star School method of computation to investigate the "feng shui luck" of any house or building:

- for each period
- for each lunar year
- and even for each lunar month

This theory is based on the assumption that the intangible forces of the earth are never constant. They are always in a state of flux. And these forces are not static, they are dynamic! These intangible forces evolve and change, and their effects on the feng shui of any structure likewise changes with time.

For this reason, serious practitioners of feng shui, especially the business community of Hong Kong have their feng shui "checked" out annually on a regular basis - not just to make sure the intangible forces of the time dimensions are accurately worked out, but also to ensure that any change in surrounding landscapes is taken note of and attended to. Feng Shui Masters in Hong Kong therefore, often work on a "retainer" basis with their many corporate and tycoon clients!

CHAPTER
FOUR

Applications
Of
Flying Star

Natal Chart
of a period
6 house

Applications of Flying Star feng shui | **Four**

CHANGING THE HOUSE FROM ONE PERIOD TO THE NEXT

This is one of the most potent applications of flying star.
If you live in an old house which was built before 1983 you can check when it was built or last renovated and then cast its natal chart. When you analyze the flying star chart, you can see if the house continues to be prosperous in this period, and if not you might want to change it into a period 7 house. Before you do it however you could then see what the stars look like if yours became a period of 7 house. If you like what you see, then you can always arrange for your house to be renovated now ie in this current period, thereby turning it into a period of 7 house. Study the examples dealt with in these following pages ...

DRAWING UP NATAL CHART OF A PERIOD 6 HOUSE
Firstly, just in case there are readers who live in houses built or last renovated before the period 7 ie between the years **1964 and 1983**, here is an example of how you would cast the natal chart for such a period of 6 house.

- Start with a Lo Shu Square with 6 as the center number.
- Determine the location of the main door. In our example it is Southwest. This makes the center star numeral of the **siang sin star** the number 3. From here we also know the **chor sin star** is 9 because 9 is in the grid directly opposite the Southwest (the location of the main door)
- Determine which subsection of the SW the door is facing – here in our example it is the second subsection. So this causes the odd numbered siang sin star numerals to move in a minus (-) mode. And this also makes the odd numbered chor sin star move in a minus mode (-)
- Now look at the period Lo Shu and work out the way the Natal chart should look ... the finished natal chart is on the right.

Natal chart of our example Period 6 house

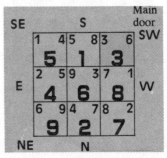

DETERMINING THE PERIOD OF YOUR HOUSE

If your house was constructed say in 1953, then according to flying star your house was " born" in that year. If between the time it was built until today the house never underwent any changes, renovations, repaint jobs – nothing at all … then the house is said to be a period of 5 house. (see page 24 for the different time periods). To cast its natal chart you would use the Lo Shu square with the number 5 in the center. But if it was extensively renovated, changed, remodeled and rebuilt then the date of the renovation would be taken as its **rebirth date**. So say it was extensively rebuilt between 1964 to 1983 this would make it a period of 6 house. If it was renovated between 1983 to the present period, it would become a period of 7 house.

WHAT CONSTITUTES A REBIRTH ?

One of the controversies between the senior Masters of Flying Star feng shui is how to determine what makes for the rebirth of a house ? It is easy to judge when there is a huge and major renovation. Then there is no doubt that the house is being extensively changed and thus being "reborn." But how big does the renovation have to be before it can be considered a rebirth that causes the house to change periods. I have discussed this point at some length with many feng shui masters. One school maintains that the roof of the building has to be changed before it can be counted as a rebirth. Another school says that a simple new coat of paint inside and outside should qualify for the rebirth and period change.

The answer lies somewhere in between. I believe that as long as there is structural change made to the house, ie when new walls get put up or knocked down, and when extensions are made should count as a rebirth. I do find it rather hard now to accept that a simple repaint job can count as a renovation.

Or that an interior decoration job can count as a renovation. Thus if you want to change the period of your house do make sure you are clear about how much work has to be done to qualify. And do check the flying star chart of your new door direction if this is being changed as part of the renovation.

CHAPTER
FOUR

Applications
Of
Flying Star

Changing the
period of your
house

CHANGING THE PERIOD OF YOUR HOUSE

Here is an example of what you should do if you are considering to improve your feng shui by changing the period of your house. This option is only for people living in houses built before 1983 ie in the period of 6 and before that. Those living in houses in this 7 period will have to wait to 2003 before they have the option of changing their houses into period of 8 houses.

Example:
Say your house was built in 1965 ie in the period of 6. The Lo Shu square will have the numeral 6 in the center. And supposing the natal chart of the house looked like the sketch shown here, with the main door located in the first subsection of the SOUTH grid and making the center siang sin star 1 (an odd number) and the center chor sin star 2 (even).

Main door is located in the FIRST subsector of SOUTH

The chor sin center numeral is 2 which is the main star numeral in the grid opposite the SOUTH ie in the North

The siang sin center numeral is 1 because the main door is located in the SOUTH which has the number 1

The flying mode of the **siang sin** star is plus (+) because the number one is odd and it represents a cardinal direction in the original Lo Shu square. Here in this example the flying mode of the **chor sin** star is also plus (+) because the **back door** is in the second subsection (as in - + + for even numbers). Based on the way these secondary stars fly, the natal chart is drawn up accordingly and shown above. Based on the chart above, the location of the main door is afflicted with the water numeral 5. This is not a good feature and is sufficient cause for the owners of the house to consider making the house into a period of 7 house by making some renovations to the house. Before doing the renovations it is useful to see what a period 7 chart will look like if there is no change to the door location and direction.

CHANGING THE PERIOD OF YOUR HOUSE ...

We have seen the natal chart in the previous page revealing the flying stars of the original period 6 at work. If we compare that with the new period 7 chart drawn up for the same house we see a dramatic difference in the feng shui luck of the house over the two "periods". Please note that this chart has been computed using exactly the same method given in Chapter 2 . the Lo shu ahs the 7 in the center because we have changed the house into a & period house.

Note in this new chart here that the main door's SOUTH sector now has the very auspicious double 7. In the period of 6 chart, this same sector had the auspicious 6 as the chor sin star but the sector was darkened by the inauspicious 5 siang sin star. That combination was not auspicious. Certainly the luck of the house was nothing compared with the excellence of the double 7 indicated for this current period.

With such a clear improvement indicated, I would definitely advise that this house be changed into a period of 7 house immediately. To benefit from the better flying stars the owner of the house should carry out at least some symbolic renovation (eg by making a new door and changing the roof.)

There is no need to make a huge renovation job to activate the **rebirth** luck. As long as there is some small structural change that would be sufficient to make the change work. In any case, maintaining the house with frequent repaint jobs brings precious yang energy into the house and is always good luck to do. I personally am always doing something to my house every year as I believe this refreshes the energy of the home substantially.

CHAPTER
FOUR

Applications
Of
Flying Star

Checking the
annual luck

Applications of Flying Star feng shui	**Four**

CHECKING THE ANNUAL LUCK OF THE HOUSE

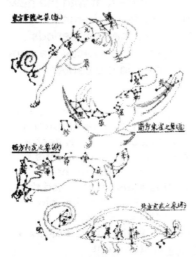

Another excellent and very useful application of flying star is to use the natal chart to investigate the annual and monthly luck of all the different sectors of the house.

In Hong Kong, many feng shui Masters specialize in doing nothing but calculating out the lucky and unlucky months of houses based on the flying star chart. Such readings are deemed to be even more useful than the Four Pillars or Purple Star astrology and fortune telling charts.

Flying star readings of houses affect the entire family. The good thing about these readings is that if something "bad" is indicated in the chart, the dates can be pinpointed very exactly using the lunar Ghanzi calendar of months.

To pinpoint good and bad coming events during the course of a calendar year, it is necessary to know how to interpret the numbers. There is thus a large section on how to interpret the numbers later in the book. But for the moment it is also necessary to know how and what to compare. We have already been introduced to the natal chart. This shows us the flying star numerals of every sector of the house . Now we also need to look at the flying star numerals of the time factor.

There are Lo shu numerals for each day, each lunar month, each lunar year and each period. These numbers are thus moving all the time and Tong Shu calculations of good days and bad days are based on these numerals. It is also possible to use flying star to compute truly auspicious days for getting married, for starting a new business, for making renovations and for doing a host of other things. I am not an expert on this branch of flying star so please don't email me to give you the auspicious dates. It is, I am told a complicated calculation !

CHECKING THE ANNUAL LUCK OF THE HOUSE ...

What you **can** get from this book however is to be able to undertake some *fortune telling* for your own house. You can investigate the annual and monthly luck of your house and office.

With your natal chart beside you, and armed also with the Lo Shu tables and charts for the coming years and months (these are presented in the following pages) , you will be able to study the patterns of numbers and from there discover which rooms will be afflicted with bad flying stars in which month and in what year. And then as they say, forewarned is for-armed. When the stars turn bad you can simply get out of the room or the house – go for vacation, plan a business trip ... or simply move temporarily to another part of the house. Where it is possible you can introduce objects to suppress the bad luck stars. Of course some stars will be harder to suppress than others. But you will discover that knowing how to check your luck will be of great assistance. This book then becomes your reference book on the tables and the numbers. And if you are clever, you can even spot the sequence and patterns of numbers and realize that you have within these pages, the key that unlocks the Lo shu numbers for time to infinity ..

Apart from being warned about bad stars you can also be alerted to the good stars that fly into your house bringing the potential for extreme good fortune. Good flying stars come as frequently as bad flying stars. And you can check these as frequently as you wish. When you know that the stars for a particular sector of the house has turned excellent you should energize that corner to magnify and embellish the good luck. The enhancement of the sectors is based almost exclusively on the wuxing or five-element theory. This embellishment of good luck lies at the core of feng shui practice. It is the true essence of what feng shui is all about.

Do note that according to flying star feng shui good luck and bad luck caused by the star numerals has a time limit which can be as short-lived as one lunar month or can be as long as twenty years and beyond. This is a dynamic practice.

CHAPTER
FOUR

Applications
Of
Flying Star

Reigning
numbers of
lunar years

| Applications of Flying Star feng shui | **Four** |

REIGNING NUMBERS OF LUNAR YEARS

Start your investigation by learning about the annual and monthly Lo Shu Tables and flying star numbers. Each lunar year has a reigning number, just as each lunar month also has a reigning number.

The annual reigning numbers move in a "reverse order" from year to year i.e. from 9 to 8 to 7 to 6 to 5 to 4 to 3 to 2 to 1 and back again to 9, and so forth. These numbers refer to the years based in the Chinese **lunar calendar**. So when we speak of a New Year with a new Lo shu reigning number, we know that the luck has changed. This "annual luck" changes in the early spring of each year just before the lunar New Year. It is therefore always advisable to appraise the feng shui in each new year on a regular basis. This makes you aware of the good and bad intangible forces that are affecting the house in the new year. For accuracy i.e. to determine the exact dates of each of the lunar new years, I usually refer to the hundred year lunar calendar with its equivalent Western and Chinese dates.

For convenience, however, it is possible to roughly express the years in accordance with the Western calendar, as long as you remember that the change in the nature of the feng shui forces take place during the lunar new year and not the western new year.

This is anywhere between the second week of January to the second week of February. With that proviso, reproduced here are the reigning numbers.

YEAR	Reigning number	YEAR	Reigning number
1998	2	2009	2
1999	1	2010	1
2000	9	2012	9
2003	8	2013	8
2004	7	2014	7
2005	6	2015	6
2006	5	2016	5
2007	4	2017	4
2008	3	2018	3

THE HUNDRED YEAR LUNAR CALENDAR

YEAR	Lunar year starts in	YEAR	Lunar year starts in
1924	Feb 5th	1960	Jan 28th
1925	Jan 24th	1961	Feb 15th
1926	Feb 13th	1962	Feb 5th
1927	Feb 2nd	1963	Jan 25th
1928	Jan 23rd	1964	Feb 13th
1929	Feb 10th	1965	Feb 2nd
1930	Jan 30th	1966	Jan 21st
1931	Feb 17th	1967	Feb 9th
1932	Feb 6th	1968	Jan 30th
1933	Jan 26th	1969	Feb 17th
1034	Feb 14th	1970	Feb 6th
1935	Feb 4th	1971	Jan 27th
1936	Jan 24th	1972	Feb 15th
1937	Feb 11th	1973	Feb 3rd
1938	Jan 31st	1974	Jan 23rd
1939	Feb 19th	1975	Feb 11th
1940	Feb 8th	1976	Jan 31st
1941	Jan 27th	1977	Feb 18th
1942	Feb 15th	1978	Feb 7th
1943	Feb 5th	1979	Jan 28th
1944	Jan 25th	1980	Feb 16th
1945	Feb 13th	1981	Feb 5th
1946	Feb 2nd	1982	Jan 25th
1947	Jan 22nd	1983	Feb 13th
1948	Feb 10th	1984	Feb 2nd
1949	Jan 29th	1985	Feb 20th
1950	Feb 17th	1986	Feb 9th
1951	Feb 6th	1987	Jan 29th
1952	Jan 27th	1988	Feb 17th
1953	Feb 14th	1989	Feb 6th
1954	Feb 3rd	1990	Jan 27th
1955	Jan 24th	1991	Feb 15th
1956	Feb 12th	1992	Feb 4th
1957	Jan 31st	1993	Jan 23rd
1958	Feb 18th	1994	Feb 10th
1959	Feb 8th	1995	Jan 31st

CHAPTER
FOUR

Applications
Of
Flying Star

The 100 year
lunar
calendar

Applications of Flying Star feng shui | **Four**

THE HUNDRED YEAR LUNAR CALENDAR

YEAR	Lunar year starts in	YEAR	Lunar year starts in
1996	Feb 19th	2002	Feb 12th
1997	Feb 7th	2003	Feb 1st
1998	Jan 28th	2004	Jan 22nd
1999	Feb 16th	2005	Feb 9th
2000	Feb 5th	2006	Jan 29th
2001	Jan 24th	2007	Feb 18th

The 100 year lunar calendar given on these two pages allows you to convert western new years into lunar new years. Thus when working out the reigning Lo shu number for the year please note that the word year in flying star feng shui refers to the lunar year which as you can see starts in the Spring.

The Lunar New Year
The New Year is considered the start of a new time, a new beginning. Usually when you have just been through an especially trying year, you can look forward to a new year when your luck can and usually does change. The readings given based on the earthly branches of the Four Pillars (ie the 12 animals readings) are at best superficial and very general. To get a proper reading of your heaven fate luck you should go to a properly qualified Master of Four Pillars or Purple Star Astrology (check **www.worldoffengshui.com** for genuine Masters who can give you a reading) . Then use flying star feng shui to get a luck reading of your house

REIGNING NUMBERS OF LUNAR MONTHS

As for the years there are also reigning numbers for each of the lunar months. The transition of the reigning Lo Shu numbers for the months from one number to the next also moves in a reverse order i.e. from 5 to 4 to 3 to 2 and so forth. Once again it is necessary to pinpoint the exact dates of the western calendar when we refer to months since the two calendar systems differ. Those keen on checking the reigning number of the *lunar month* should consult the Chinese calendar and then extrapolate the relevant Lo-Shu number for the month accordingly.

To get you started, the first month of this year of the Rabbit (**1999**) begins on February 16th and ends on 17th March. The reigning Lo-Shu number for this first month of this year 1999 was the number 8.

- for the second month (18th mar to 15th april) the number is 7
- for the third month (16th april to 14th may) the number is 6
- for the fourth month (15th may to 13th june) the number is 5
- for the fifth month (14th june to 12th july) the number is 4

- for the sixth month (13th july to 10th august) the number is 3
- for the seventh month (11th aug to 9th sept.) the number is 2
- for the eighth month (10th sept to 8th oct) the number is 1
- for the ninth month (9th oct to 7th nov) the number is 9

- for the tenth month (8th nov to 7th dec) the number is 8
- for the eleventh month (8th dec to 6th jan) the number is 7
- for the twelfth month (7th jan 2000 to 4th feb) the number is 6

The method of investigating the flying star of a house or building in any given year is to draw up the twelve month charts, so that the progression of the star numerals as they change from month to month can be tracked The feng shui of houses and buildings can thus be charted in the same way that personal horoscopes are drawn up. Reading and analysing time dimension feng shui, (like personal horoscope readings under the Chinese system) is based on the **five element relationship** analysis and on the meanings of the star numerals and their combinations.

CHAPTER
FOUR

Applications
Of
Flying Star

Putting year
and months
together

Applications of Flying Star feng shui | Four

PUTTING YEAR AND MONTHS TOGETHER

To chart the monthly "feng shui luck" of a house or building over one calendar year, here is what you should do step by step:

- First you select the **year** under investigation.
- Then you determine the **reigning Lo shu number** for that year which enables you to select the **relevant Lo shu grid**. Thus if the year being investigated is 1999, note that the reigning number for 1999 is I so what we need is the Lo Shu square which has the number 1 in the center. The arrangement of the numbers in a Lo shu 1 square is illustrated below. Note the sequence of the numbers in all the squares. Note also that in keeping with the tradition of authentic feng shui books, the direction south is always placed on top in the illustration. In real life the compass determines all the directions.

This is the Lo shu square for the **YEAR 1999** which has the 1 in the center.

south		
9	5	7
8	1	3
4	6	2

- These numbers represent the **year stars**. They are shown as the big numerals in the center. The Lo Shu number of the year is in the center.
- Next you must look at the monthly Lo Shu grids which show the numbers for each month. The Lo Shu number for the month is placed in the center, and the other numbers follow from this center number.
- Place the month numbers next to the annual numbers. Follow the sequence of the flight path. This is the chart for the month.
- Use this chart to compare with the house natal chart. Study all the numbers grid by grid. Examine the grid where the door is located and look at all the numbers in that grid. Then go to the chapter with the meanings of the numbers to give you a reading of the luck of your main door in that month. Try to find months that are exceptionally good – that is the month when you should invest, start a business, and take some risks. When the month is bad simply lie low.

MONTHLY FLYING STAR CHARTS FOR 1999

Here and in the following two pages are monthly flying star charts for the twelve lunar months of 1999. You can see that the numbers combine differently each month with the year numbers. Note the combinations of double 5s and 2/5s as these are the numerals to beware of. In the grids where these combinations appear, check against the natal chart and beware of there being 2s or 5s in the same grid.

9^7	5^3	7^5
8^6	1^8	3^1
4^2	6^4	2^9

First month:
16th Feb to 17th March 1999

9^6	5^2	7^4
8^5	1^7	3^9
4^1	6^3	2^8

Second month:
18th March to 15th April 1999

9^5	5^1	7^3
8^4	1^6	3^8
4^9	6^2	2^7

Third month:
16th April to 14th May 1999

9^4	5^9	7^2
8^3	1^5	3^7
4^8	6^1	2^6

Fourth month:
15th May to 13th June 1999

CHAPTER
FOUR

Applications
Of
Flying Star

The monthly
flying chart
for **1999**

Applications of Flying Star feng shui — **Four**

MONTHLY FLYING STAR CHARTS FOR 1999 continued …
Whenever you notice a collection of 2s and 5s coming altogether in one
sector or grid, the flying stars are giving you a very loud warning that
something very bad is going to happen that will affect the person staying
or sleeping in that corner. Usually a preponderance of 5s indicate a
serious accident or health problem ripening.

9^3	5^8	7^1
8^2	1^4	3^6
4^7	6^9	2^5

Fifth month:
14th June to 12th June 1999

9^2	5^7	7^9
8^1	1^3	3^5
4^6	6^8	2^4

Sixth month:
13th July to 10th August 1999

9^1	5^6	7^8
8^9	1^2	3^4
4^5	6^7	2^3

Seventh month:
11th August to 9th Sept 1999

9^9	5^5	7^7
8^8	1^1	3^3
4^4	6^6	2^2

Eighth month:
10th Sept to 8th Oct 1999

MONTHLY FLYING STAR CHARTS FOR 1999 continued ...
Another nasty combination, which creates misunderstandings, high
tempers and a great deal of unhappiness is the 2/3 or 3/2 combination.
When this is compounded by similar occurrence of these numerals in the
same grid of the House natal chart, it is advisable to immediately do
something about it. Otherwise simple anger could well lead to violence.

9^8	5^4	7^6
8^7	1^9	3^2
4^3	6^5	2^1

Ninth month:
9th Oct to 7th Nov 1999

9^7	5^3	7^5
8^6	1^8	3^1
4^2	6^4	2^9

Tenth month:
8th Nov to 7th Dec 1999

9^6	5^2	7^4
8^5	1^7	3^9
4^1	6^3	2^8

Eleventh month:
8th December to 6th Jan 1999

9^5	5^1	7^3
8^4	1^6	3^8
4^9	6^2	2^7

Twelfth month:
7th Jan to 4th Feb 1999

CHAPTER
FOUR

Applications
Of
Flying Star

The monthly
flying chart
for **2000**

Applications of Flying Star feng shui | **Four**

MONTHLY FLYING STAR CHARTS FOR 2000
In the year 2000 note that the Lo Shu square ahs changed and the center number is now **9** . The good star combinations to look out for are the occurrence of the 7s during this period. This number is lucky only in this period. When we reach the year 2003 and change to the period of 8 the number 7 is no longer regarded an auspicious star numeral.

8^4	4^9	6^2
7^3	9^5	2^7
3^8	5^1	1^6

First month:
5th Feb to 5th March 2000

8^3	4^8	6^1
7^2	9^4	2^6
3^7	5^9	1^5

Second month:
6th Mar to 4th April 2000

8^2	4^7	6^9
7^1	9^3	2^5
3^6	5^8	1^4

Third month:
5th April to 3rd May 2000

8^1	4^6	6^8
7^9	9^2	2^4
3^5	5^7	1^3

Fourth month:
4th May to 1st June 2000

MONTHLY FLYING STAR CHARTS FOR 2000 continued …
When you check these monthly Lo shu charts always remember that the
top center grid always represent the South. This is the traditional way of
presenting the Lo Shu charts found in the old books. These monthly charts
are the Lo shu numerals that apply to everything and to every city and
country, even to the stock market of countries !

8^9	4^5	6^7
7^8	9^1	2^3
3^4	5^6	1^2

Fifth month:
2nd June to 1st July 2000

8^8	4^4	6^6
7^7	9^9	2^2
3^3	5^5	1^1

Sixth month:
2nd July to 30th July 2000

8^7	4^3	6^5
7^6	9^8	2^1
3^2	5^4	1^9

Seventh month:
31st July to 28th August 2000

8^6	4^2	6^4
7^5	9^7	2^9
3^1	5^3	1^8

Eighth month:
29th August to 27th Sept 2000

CHAPTER
FOUR

Applications
Of
Flying Star

The monthly
flying chart
for **2000**

Applications of Flying Star feng shui | **Four**

MONTHLY FLYING STAR CHARTS FOR 2000 continued …
The way to use these charts for larger areas like countries and continents
is to visualize superimposing the Lo shu square onto the map of a country
or continent. The chart will tell you which part of the country will have
severe bad luck or good luck eg. When an epidemic might break out or
when an economic crisis might take place.

8^5	4^1	6^3
7^4	9^6	2^8
3^9	5^2	1^7

Ninth month:
28th Sept to 26th Oct 2000

8^4	4^9	6^2
7^3	9^5	2^7
3^8	5^1	1^6

Tenth month:
27th Oct to 25th Nov 2000

8^3	4^8	6^1
7^2	9^4	2^6
3^7	5^9	1^5

Eleventh month:
26th Nov to 25th Dec 2000

8^2	4^7	6^9
7^1	9^3	2^5
3^6	5^8	1^4

Twelfth month:
26th August to 23rd Jan 2000

MONTHLY FLYING STAR CHARTS FOR 2001
Note once again that we are changing the main star numerals because the Lo shu grid for 2001 has now changed and the center number is 8. By now also you should be observing the way the numbers fly around the grid. Both the annual and monthly numbers move in an ascending mode. From this sequence it is not difficult to work out the numbers for future years.

7^1	3^6	5^8
6^9	8^2	1^4
2^5	4^7	9^3

First month:
24th Jan to 22nd Feb 2001

7^9	3^5	5^7
6^8	8^1	1^3
2^4	4^6	9^2

Second month:
23rd Feb to 24th march 2001

7^8	3^4	5^6
6^7	8^9	1^2
2^3	4^5	9^1

Third month:
25th March to 22nd April 2001

7^7	3^3	5^5
6^6	8^8	1^1
2^2	4^4	9^9

Fourth and Fifth month:
23rd April to 20th June 2001

CHAPTER
FOUR

Applications
Of
Flying Star

The monthly
flying chart
for **2001**

Applications of Flying Star feng shui | **Four**

MONTHLY FLYING STAR CHARTS FOR 2001 continued …
It should be becoming clear that the most important grid to investigate is where the main door is located. When the numbers in this grid are bad, the whole house gets afflicted. And when the stars are auspicious likewise the entire house benefits. So always check the main door grid because this indicates good or bad luck for the house.

7^6	3^2	5^4
6^5	8^7	1^9
2^1	4^3	9^8

Sixth month:
21st June to 20th July 2001

7^5	3^1	5^3
6^4	8^6	1^8
2^9	4^2	9^7

Seventh month:
21st July to 18th Sept 2001

7^4	3^9	5^2
6^3	8^5	1^7
2^8	4^1	9^6

Eighth month:
19th August to 16th Sept 2001

7^3	3^8	5^1
6^2	8^4	1^6
2^7	4^9	9^5

Ninth month:
17th Sept to 16th Oct 2001

MONTHLY FLYING STAR CHARTS FOR 2001 continued …
In this part of flying star we have not mentioned the siang sin and chor sin stars. This does not mean they do not exert their influence. Indeed it is when these stars have bad numbers and then are combined with the bad stars of the month and year that severe misfortune occurs. How severe depedns on the which grid is being studied.

7^2	3^7	5^9
6^1	8^3	1^5
2^6	4^8	9^4

Tenth month:
17th Oct to 14th Nov 2001

7^1	3^6	5^8
6^9	8^2	1^4
2^5	4^7	9^3

Eleventh month:
15th Nov to 14th Dec 2001

7^9	3^5	5^7
6^8	8^1	1^3
2^4	4^6	9^2

Twelveth month:
15th Dec to 12th Jan 2001

7^8	3^4	5^6
6^7	8^9	1^2
2^3	4^5	9^1

Thirteenth month:
13th Jan to 11th Feb 2001

CHAPTER
FOUR

Applications
Of
Flying Star

The monthly
flying chart
for **2002**

Applications of Flying Star feng shui | Four

MONTHLY FLYING STAR CHARTS FOR 2002

In addition to spotting obvious bad (2,5)and auspicious numbers (1,6,8) there is also the Element aspect of the analysis of the numbers. In many ways this requires the most skillful part of the application of flying star. Good feng shui Consultants are those who have a deep understanding of the correlation between the elements and the numbers.

6^7	2^3	4^5
5^6	7^8	9^1
1^2	3^4	8^9

First month:
12th Feb to 13th March 2002

6^6	2^2	4^4
5^5	7^7	9^9
1^1	3^3	8^8

Second month:
14th March to 12th April 2002

6^7	2^3	4^5
5^6	7^8	9^1
1^2	3^4	8^9

Third month:
13th April to 11th May 2002

6^7	2^3	4^5
5^6	7^8	9^1
1^2	3^4	8^9

Fourth month:
12th May to 1oth June 2002

MONTHLY FLYING STAR CHARTS FOR 2002 continued …
The monthly Lo Shu charts illustrated here have been presented in a way which enables the first time practitioner to get the hang of undertaking a flying star reading. By now it should be easy for anyone to work out the Lo Shu flying star charts themselves using the reigning numbers for the center of the grids. The secret is to note the flight path of the numbers.

6^3	2^8	4^1
5^2	7^4	9^6
1^7	3^9	8^5

Fifth month:
11th June to 9th July 2002

6^2	2^7	4^9
5^1	7^3	9^5
1^6	3^8	8^4

Sixth month:
10th July to 8th August 2002

6^1	2^6	4^8
5^9	7^2	9^4
1^5	3^7	8^3

Seventh month:
19th August to 6th Sept 2002

6^9	2^5	4^7
5^8	7^1	9^3
1^4	3^6	8^2

Eighth month:
7th Sept to 5th Oct 2002

CHAPTER
FOUR

Applications
Of
Flying Star

Monthly
Lo Shu
numbers to
2004

Applications of Flying Star feng shui | **Four**

Using these Lo shu numbers, make an attempt to draw up the relevant Lo Shu flying star charts for the following months.

MONTHLY LO SHU NUMBERS FOR LUNAR YEAR 2002
Seventh month: 9th Aug to 6th Sept - Lo-Shu number 2
Eighth month: 7th Sept to 5th Oct - Lo-Shu number 1
Ninth month: 6th Oct to 4th Nov - Lo-Shu number 9
Tenth month: 5th Nov to 3rd Dec - Lo-Shu number 8
Eleventh month: 4th Dec to 2nd Jan - Lo-Shu number 7
Twelfth month: 3rd Jan '95 to 31st Jan - Lo-Shu number 6

MONTHLY LO SHU NUMBERS FOR LUNAR YEAR 2003
First month: 1st Feb to 2nd Mar - Lo-Shu number 5
Second month: 3rd Mar to 1st Apr - Lo-Shu number 4
Third month: 2nd Apr to 30th Apr - Lo-Shu number 3
Fourth month: 1st May to 30th May - Lo-Shu number 2
Fifth month: 31st May to 29th Jun - Lo-Shu number 1
Sixth month: 30th Jun to 28th Jul - Lo-Shu number 9
Seventh month: 29th Jul to 27th Aug - Lo-Shu number 8
Eighth month: 28th Aug to 25th Sep - Lo-Shu number 7
Ninth month: 26th Sep to 24th Oct - Lo-Shu number 6
Tenth month: 25th Oct - 23rd Nov - Lo-Shu number 5
Eleventh month: 24th Nov to 22nd Dec - Lo-Shu number 4
Twelfth month: 23rd Dec to 21st Jan - Lo-Shu number 3

MONTHLY LO SHU NUMBERS FOR LUNAR YEAR 2004

First month: 22nd Jan to 19th Feb - Lo-Shu number 2
Second/Third months: 20th Feb to 18th Apr - Lo-Shu number 1
Fourth month: 19th Apr to 18th May - Lo-Shu number 9
Fifth month: 19th May to 17th Jun - Lo-Shu number 8
Sixth month: 18th Jun to 16th Jul - Lo-Shu number 7
Seventh month: 17th Jul to 15th Aug - Lo-Shu number 6
Eighth month: 16th Aug to 13th Sep - Lo-Shu number 5
Ninth month: 14th Sep to 13th Oct - Lo-Shu number 4
Tenth month: 14th Oct to 11th Nov - Lo-Shu number 3
Eleventh month: 12th Nov to 11th Dec - Lo-Shu number 2
Twelfth month: 12th Dec to 9th Jan 2005 - Lo-Shu number 1
Thirteenth month: 10th Jan to 8th Feb 2005 - Lo-Shu number 9

The Lake has risen up to Heaven...

The lake has risen up to heaven
The image of breakthrough
Thus the superior man dispenses his riches downward
And refrains from resting on his virtue.

From the I CHING on the hexagram Kuai (Resoluteness)

Chapter Five
The meanings of the Numbers

The waters manifest union of movement and strength
The superior man knows
Perseverance brings good fortune

From the I CHING on the
Hexagram Ta Chuang – the Power of the Great

The Meanings of the Numbers	Five

With flying star feng shui analyses, auspicious star numbers can be activated to magnify good fortune and inauspicious numbers can be dissolved to reduce the effects of misfortune. Knowledge and appreciation of the five elements and their interactive relationships is vital in this part of the practice. Incorporating flying star into the overall practice of feng shui makes it more complete and also more accurate.

This is because understanding the method ensures that one does not inadvertently "activate" an unlucky combination of numbers, which can happen, when one unknowingly strengthens the ill effects of certain star numbers. For instance, you may be activating your wealth corner - the South East - based on the Eight Aspirations method of feng shui, and of course it will work. But the flying stars may be afflicting the sector in a certain month of a certain year and energizing the wood of the SE in that month could cause misfortune brought by flying stars to get increased. It is advisable to be careful…

I made this mistake once when activating for good business luck prior to a business trip. I placed a windchime in the Northwest sector. I had a successful business trip but discovered that in my absence, my staff and an important client had quarreled violently. A most unpleasant situation had developed. Puzzled, I checked my flying star numbers immediately and discovered to my horror that I had a 3/2 star in the NW that month. This troublesome set of numbers had been badly exacerbated by the noisy windchime, which I had put there to energize business luck.

Thus while the windchime did help me in my business trip, it had also made the 3/2 combination of flying stars a lot worse as a result of which I nearly lost both my client and my very wonderful employee. I removed the windchime at once and placed an urn of still water in that corner in an attempt to soothe the noisy energies of the sector. Things became better almost as soon as I removed the chimes.

It is thus absolutely necessary to understand the meanings of numbers and their combinations. It is also necessary to know what to do to nullify bad effects or to transform bad energy brought by bad stars into good energy.

CHAPTER
FIVE

The
Meanings
of the
Numbers

The
Auspicious
numbers

The Meanings of the Numbers | Five

The meanings attributed to the numbers 1 to 9 have been extracted from several old Chinese Manuals and simplified for ease of application. You can use them to interpret the auspicious and inauspicious sectors of any home or building for this period of 7 (1984 to 2003) or for any period in the coming years. To obtain the relevant Lo-Shu of Period 7 houses, and also the Lo Shu for different years and even the different months, please refer to the charts and tables already given in the preceding chapters.

The AUSPICIOUS NUMBERS
The most auspcious numbers are said to be the reigning number of the relevant period, year or month, as well as the numbers 1, 6 and 8.

The **number 1** represents long gone prosperity. But because it represents water, and water means wealth or money it is regarded favorably. In fact the number often denotes the start of a new beginning. It symbolizes things getting better after having been bad. The number 1 in a siang sin star is especially auspcious.

The **number 6** represents faded prosperity, but because it symbolizes the Trigram Chien, which means gold it also means riches and prosperity. In fcat the number 6 is highly prized and everytime it occurs in the NW sector, the Patrircah of the home benefits and is said to be going through a good period.

The **number 8** represents future prosperity because it is the reigning number of the next period. It is also regarded as a very lucky number which will continue to be lucky for the forthcoming 20 years.

The **number 7** represents current prosperity and when 7 falls in that sector of one's house which has open spaces and/or where the entrance or main door is located the symbolism is most auspciious. Because 7 is such an important number between now and the year 2003, it should be activated by placing a clock, a pendulum or any other moving object in the center of the house which has 7 during this period. If the two stars, the siang sin and the chor sin have 7 in the sector of your main door, it is a very auspicious indication which can also be magnified and enhanced in several different ways.

The number 9 represents distant prosperity. This is because 9 is the reigning number of the 20 year period of the distant future i.e. from the years 2024 to 2043 in the next century. But 9 is always a lucky number irrespective of the period. Much like 8, this number is a perreniel favourite with the Chinese. The number 9 denotes the fire element and is esepcially auspicious when it occurs as a mountain chor sin flown into either of the earth sectors Southwest or North east. The number 9 is alo a number tha cannot change or be corrupted. Irrspective of how many times you multiply 9 by, the sum of its digits always add up to 9.

The **UNLUCKY NUMBERS**

The two numbers to be very wary of in flying star are the numbers **5** and **2**. Both these numbers represent the Earth element based on thc Later Heaven Pa-Kua arrangement of Trigrams and Elements. According to the manuals, these numbers are said to bring grave misfortune and sickness to whoever is occupying the grids into which they fall. Thus, they should always be strongly resisted with suitable feng shui tools.

These two numbers are said to create Shar Chi caused by intangible forces, similar to, and sometimes more lethal than those created by physical poison arrows. Illness and fatal accidents are caused by 5 and 2. They must therefore be resisted wherever they appear as star numbers in the chart.

To combat that pernicious effect of 5 use a five rod windchime to exhaust the energy generated by its earth element at the location having the 5 influence during the relevant period. The windchime's sounds will create the Metal energy necessary to exhaust the Earth. Another stronger method is to hang a curved knife high up near the ceiling which symbolically destroys the 5 star.

To dissolve the bad effects of 2, hang a string of six metal coins at the location having the 2 influence in the relevant period. Again this is because Metal exhausts the Earth of 2. The number 6 (and thus the 6 coins) represents Chien or big metal in the Pa-Kua symbol. The effect is extremely powerful since 6 also represents the power of heavenly forces. A 6 rod winchime is also effective. If both 5 and 2 occur together use a larger windchime to add strength.

CHAPTER
FIVE

The
Meanings
of the
Numbers

The Bad
Combined
Numbers

The Meanings of the Numbers | Five

THE INAUSPICIOUS COMBINED NUMBERS

The Manuals also set out the meanings of combined numbers when they appear together in any one sector, as the siang sin star number and as the chor sin star number. Thus

- When the **2** and **2** occur together there will be chronic illness for any person who lives, works or sleeps in that sector. A mountain star 2 is said to be a severely afflicted star, and when this occurs in the south sector the severity is increased again. In the wood sectors East and Southeast the mountain star 2 is not as severe as in the South. A 2 water star cause things to rot and go bad. Illness caused by such a star usually has to do with tumors and cancers. The 2 can also occur as the main period star, as the monthly star or as the annual star. If you have a room afflicted by a double or triple 2, either move out during the period when the proliferation of 2s occur or place a very large and healthy plant in that corner that is afflicted. This is not a solution that is workable in the bedroom.
- When the number 5 occurs together as a double or triple, the effect is said to be more unlucky and more severe than 2. Manifestations of misfortune usually come as illness that is often fatal. Heart attacks, strokes and other serious health problems are indicated. Use a curved knife to counter or a 5-rod windchime but the best solution is to move out of the room when the 5's descend in.
- When 2 and 5 occur together anyone staying or working in the sector having this combination will fall ill or meet with a fatal accident. The lethal effect of this combination cannot be overstressed, but these bad effects can be overcome fi you place strong antidotes. If you do not have the curved knife try placing a large urn filled with water or a symbolic metal pagoda to " capture " the bad flying stars.

These antidotes need be in place only for the duration of the flying stars stay in the sector. Once they fly out again, it is important to bring down the " antidote" since there is nothing further to counter. Curved knives and bowls of water can themselves cause problems if you do not use them correctly. But for overcoming afflicted flying stars 2 and 5 they are quite effective.

THE INAUSPICIOUS COMBINED NUMBERS ...

- When the **2** and **3** occur together in a sector it is like a bullfighting ring/ there is plenty of bad feelings, anger and tempers created. There will be quarrels sometimes even leading to lawsuits for members of the household who occupy the afflicted sector. There will be plenty of aggressiveness leading to unpleasant consequences. Whenever you see this combination, you can safely hazard a guess that relationships between husband and wife is one of constant bickering. Likewise it also indicates problems between parents and children and between the siblings of the family. To see which family gets affected the most, just check where this combination of numbers takes place. In the SW It affects the relationships of the Mother. In the NW it affects the father. In the eats it affects the sons and in the wets it affects the daughters.

The best way to deal with this very inauspicious combination is to use the lethal combination of fire and water elements which together produces powerful steam capable of annihilating the 3 of wood and the 2 of earth. Instead of lights however use incense and place an urn of water. These two elements are deemed to have quiet strength. Burn strong pungent incense. If you can, try to obtain incense made from grass and herbs from the high mountains such as the Himalayas mountain range. These are pure and effective.

You must beware this 3/2 combination if you are in politics and business. This combination is what cause intense politicking in the office and against you. If your bedroom is in the afflicted sector, it might be a good idea to change rooms for a short while. Incense will help.
You should never have noisy or moving objects placed in a sector which has the 3/2 combination. Objects like TV sets, windchimes, bells, radios will make the negative effect a lot worse. Let the corner stay as still and as silent as possible. This is one way of making any active politicking against you die down. Do not use Pa Kua mirrors or other standard antidotes to overcome this bad flying star.

CHAPTER
FIVE

The
Meanings
of the
Numbers

The Bad
Combined
Numbers

The Meanings of the Numbers | **Five**

THE INAUSPICIOUS COMBINED NUMBERS ...

- When the **6** and **7** occur together in a sector the symbol created is " crossing swords". This combination of two metal elements suggest that anyone staying in the sector occupied by the combination will suffer a loss of income or be cheated or robbed. The energy that manifests is very shar or very killing. However, during this period of 7 (1984 to 2003) the ill effects of this combination is not so serious as it will be during the period of 8. This is because in this period the number 7 is considered to be auspicious. Nevertheless the symbol of two metal element numbers is to be viewed with care. Place a bright light in the sector to symbolically "control' the metal. Keep affected sectors well lighted. Or place something red in that corner.

If this sector afflicted by 6 and 7 happen to be the sector which houses your main front door, hang a painting of a fierce protective animal outside to symbolically stand guard against robberies and burglars. A tiger picture will be excellent. Or you can use any of the other traditional symbols of protection – stone lions, leopards, eagles, prickly cactus plants and so forth.

- The **3** and **7** combination is also said by some masters to have the same effect as the 6/7 combination, and even though it adds up to the auspicious 10, it is recommended that if you have this combination in your main door sector, use the above protective precaution.
- The **2** and **7** represents "excessive heat" and is said to cause illness due to heatinesss. Examples are high fever, high blood pressure and so forth. When these two star numbers occur together you must be careful of fire. Make sure you do not have open fires (candles and cooking stove) in that sector. Alleviate the ill effect by cooling down with water. An urn of water will do it.

THE AUSPICIOUS COMBINED NUMBERS ...

The combinations of star numbers which bring a great deal of good fortune, happiness, money luck, name, fame, recognition and cause for celebration include the following excellent combinations:

- The **6** with the **8, 1, 4** and **6** doubled
- The **8** with the **6, 1**, and **8** doubled
- The **1** with **6,8, 4** and **1** doubled

The Double 7
In addition to these traditionally auspicious combinations, the **double 7** is also regarded as being extremely auspicious during this period of 7. In other periods the number 7 is considered to be inauspicious. Thus from now until 2003, 7 stays very lucky.

If the double 7 appears in the sector of your front door, it means you will enjoy a great deal of money and success luck during the period of 7. If it is the sector which houses your back door, it is also auspicious but in this case the good luck benefits the next generation ie the children of the household. If you are fortunate enough to be able to benefit from the double 7 flying star, you can activate the good fortune even further with water and windchimes or other objects and symbols of good fortune. Anything that symbolizes activity and movement will "move" the energy and will stir the chi into action.

If you have the **double 7** in your main door sector keep the dragon fish or arrowana in an aquarium or pond to enhance your luck. Shown here is the red arrowana

Those of you currently enjoying the double 7 for your front door, remember to make changes by the year 2003.

CHAPTER
FIVE

The
Meanings
of the
Numbers

The
Siang sin

The Meanings of the Numbers | Five

THE SIANG SIN ... or Water Star

Literally this means the "direction star" which refers to the direction you face. In the north for instance the siang sin faces north and in the south it faces south, and so on. It is also referred to as the water star because a siang sin, which carries an auspicious number, should face some water for the good fortune to manifest. Water is supposed to enhance the siang sin.

Example: If the main door of your house faces North and it is located in the North sector, and the siang sin in that sector carries the auspicious number 8 (which means future prosperity), then if your front door also faces a small water feature like a pond, the door becomes auspicious. The water feature can also be a small waterfall or merely an urn full of water. Or if this same door faces an empty piece of land, which represents the "bright hall", then favourable chi is encouraged to flow into the house through the front door. This is because the favourable chi is given a chance to settle and accumulate before entering the house. A fortunate siang sin star is always more potent if it is located in a part of the building which is open, fluid, active and in a state of flux. Only then can it be relied upon to bring wealth and prosperity to the residents of the building. Any solid object, a building or a wall should never block an auspicious siang sin. If it is blocked, feng shui Masters refer to the siang sin as having been pressed down which creates bad feng shui. There will then be adverse effects on the wealth and health of residents.

Unlucky siang sin are those that carry inauspicious numbers and their presence in any sector indicates that those sectors should NOT have any water features. It is always preferred to have unlucky siang sin stars under control or pressed down. Placing heavy objects like large stones, boulders, and heavy furniture does this. Usually if the siang sin of the grid housing the front door is an unlucky number the entire house gets afflicted, and everyone in the house suffers. But by placing a heavy boulder preferably tied with red thread to be energized, the impact of the unlucky siang sin will be considerably lessened.

Another way of dealing with such a problem is to look for an alternative door to use.

THE CHOR SIN ... or Mountain Star

Literally this means the "sitting star". Thus in the north the chor sin sits and faces south the opposite direction. In the east the chor sin sits and faces west. This star is also referred to as the mountain star. In the Lo Shu natal chart the chor sin is always placed on the left hand side of the mains tar numeral while the siang sin is always placed to the right.

The chor sin should always have something large and solid to sit on. It can only be activated to bring good luck only if it is " sitting on a mountain". In feng shui terms this can be symbolized by a wall, or by something high or solid, and preferably closed. An auspicious chor sin is one that carries the numbers 1, 6, 7 or 8. If the chor sin of the grids which house the front and back door are auspicious then the luck of the house is said to be as solid as a mountain.

The chor sin should never face water since this is "mountain falling into water" which is considered inauspicious. If the number of the chor sin is itself unlucky however then allowing it to fall into the water dissolves the bad luck of the bad number. Having said this it is important to consider the combination of chor sin and siang sin numbers.

Example: we come back to the double & when both the siang sin and chor sin are deemed auspicious. Will having a water feature to energize the siang sin hurt the chor sin in any way ?

The answer is NO if the water feature is placed "facing" the siang sin. Remember that the chor sin sits and looks in the opposite direction so that energizing with a water feature to benefic the siang sin cannot possibly hurt the chor sin. The nature of these two stars is really very different and appreciating these differences greatly facilitates correct practice

Where both stars are unfortunate then the bad stars must be pressed heavily down. This can be done with a heavy object but the best way to press down on the bad luck is with the placement of a kitchen or toilet in that sector.

CHAPTER
FIVE

The
Meanings
of the
Numbers

The
Grand Duke
Jupiter

| Taking note of special situations | **Five** |

THE GRAND DUKE JUPITER ...

If you are thinking of making renovations to your house that involve banging, and breaking down walls you should take note of the GRAND DUKE JUPITER. His place of residence each year changes but wherever he is it is important that you should not disturb him with loud banging and construction. Upsetting the Grand Duke brings bad luck. Thus the first thing to take note of is to find out where he is located in each lunar year.

There are specific guidelines on how one can improve one's feng shui if one is able to garner the support and assistance of the Grand Duke. It is also vital that one should never incur the wrath of the Grand Duke. To find out the Grand Duke's location each year refer to the Table reproduced below.

In the year of the	The lunar years ...			Grand Duke Jupiter is located in
RAT		2008	2020	NORTH
OX		2009	2021	NORTH-NORTH-EAST
TIGER		2010	2022	EAST-NORTH-EAST
RABBIT	1999	2011	2023	EAST
DRAGON	2000	2012	2024	EAST-SOUTH-EAST
SNAKE	2001	2013	2025	SOUTH-SOUTH-EAST
HORSE	2002	2014	2026	SOUTH
SHEEP	2003	2015	2027	SOUTH-SOUTH-WEST
MONKEY	2004	2016	2028	WEST-SOUTH-WEST
ROOSTER	2005	2017	2029	WEST
DOG	2006	2018	2030	WEST-NORTHWEST
BOAR	2007	2019	2031	NORTH-NORTHWEST

Always remember that you **must never confront the Grand Duke** Jupiter. Thus in any year always check where the Grand Duke is and in that year make sure you do not sit facing that direction. Even if that is your best direction, you must not sit in that direction in that year.

GUIDELINES ON THE GRAND DUKE JUPITER ...

- Remember never to sit in a position that requires you to directly confront the Grand Duke. Thus in 1999 the Grand Duke is located in the East. This means you not sit in the West directly facing East. Even if you discover that East is your best location based on the EIGHT MANSIONS formula in the year 1999 you simply cannot use your best direction. If you directly confront the Grand Duke you will meet with loss, failure and problems.

- For your house, knowing where the Grand Duke is located helps ensure that you do not disturb him by having renovations or construction activity in his sector. Thus in 1999 you must not undertake any renovation in the East sector of your house since this will disturb the Grand Duke. You must postpone any planned renovations to the following year. To break this rule is to invite misfortune. The Grand Duke does not like being disturbed or touched in any way.

- And never ever confront the grand Duke in other ways. Old Chinese warlords always avoided advancing towards the enemy if it meant moving in a direction that represented the Grand Duke's location for that year. They always preferred to engage in battle with the Grand Duke behind them rather than in front of them. Thus in 1999, if you have to attend an important meeting or negotiation do not sit facing the east. Instead sit with the EAST directly behind you. This way the Grand Duke will be supporting you.

Example of the GULF WAR

In 1991 when Saddam Hussein's forces were pitted against the Allied forces of the West, the position of the Grand Duke favoured the allies. In that year the Grand Duke was located in the SOUTHWEST. The allies had their base in Saudi Arabia and when they were ready to engage in battle with the Iraqi soldiers, the Allies advanced towards KUWAIT **from the southwest thus having the Grand Duke behind them. This was a favourable orientation for them in that year.**

Saddam's forces advanced towards the Southwest thus directly confronting the Grand Duke. This was extremely inauspicious for Saddam Hussein.
The feng shui of the Allies was thus superior to the feng shui of Saddam Hussein in that year. Their victory was thus aided by feng shui.

CHAPTER
FIVE

The
Meanings
of the
Numbers

The
Three
Killings

| Taking note of special situations | **Five** |

THE THREE KILLINGS or SARM SAAT ...

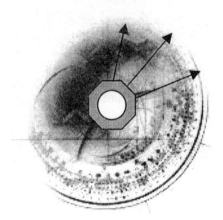

In addition to the Grand Duke Jupiter, it is also necessary to take note of the place of the *Sarm Saat* or literally the place of the Three Killings. This is a location of conflict with the Grand Duke Jupiter and it is a location that should be avoided.

Before looking at the RULES that pertain to the Sarm Saat, first take note of where its location is in each year. This is summarized in the Table.

In the years of the following animals ...	The Sarm Saat location is
OX, ROOSTER, SNAKE	EAST
BOAR, RABBIT, SHEEP	WEST
MONKEY, RAT, DRAGON	SOUTH
DOG, HORSE, TIGER	NORTH

- You must never have the Saam Saat or Three Killings behind you in any year. Thus in 1999 in the year of the Rabbit, you must not sit with the direction West behind you. This means you should not sit facing East. You may however face the Three Killings directly. This means that in 1999 you can sit facing West. Confronting the Three Killings will not hurt you but having it behind you will. In the year of the Dragon in 2000 the Three Killings is in the South so in that year, the millennium year you must not sit with the south behind you. It is far more advantageous to sit directly facing South thereby facing the Three Killings head on.

- When you are planning to do house repairs and renovations you must not do it in sectors that house the Three Killings. Thus in 1999 this means you should not undertake any renovations in the west sector of your house You may however undertake renovations in sectors that are opposite the Three Killings.

- Please note that at all times you must follow both this and the guidelines on the Grand Duke...these are simply the precautions to take when undertaking renovations.

THE DEADLY FIVE YELLOWS...

The third direction to check every year is the direction of the deadly FIVE YELLOWS. This also moves around and changes each year. This is a direction that cause a great deal of problems and it must be strongly dealt with each year.

The best way to counter the bad luck and misfortunes of the 5Yellows is to use a 5 rod windchime especially one that has a pagoda design factored in. There should also be tiny bells to dissolve the bad energy of the 5 yellows. This is illustrated in the picture here. The locations of the 5 yellows is summarized in the table here.

In the year	The Five Yellows is in ...	In the year	The Five Yellows is in ...
1999	SOUTH	2004	CENTER
2000	NORTH	2005	NORTHWEST
2001	SOUTHWEST	2006	WEST
2002	EAST	2007	NORTHEAST
2003	SOUTHEAST	2008	SOUTH

- The guideline on the5 yellows is that you must not undertake any renovations where it is located. Thus if you are planning to have a new kitchen and the Five yellows is located in the kitchen. It is best to postpone the renovation until the following year when the Five Yellows has flown into another grid. In the lunar year1999 the location of this harmful manifestation of bad energy is the South. This also means that the South is generally afflicted during the year. Use a windchime to overcome it. Please note that if you are making massive renovations that involve the entire house then the taboos on all three manifestations- the Grand Duke, the Three Killings and the Five yellows no longer apply.

CHAPTER
FIVE

The
Meanings
of the
Numbers

The
Nine Star
Colours

Taking note of special situations | **Five**

THE NINE STAR COLOURS

A supplementary text on the meanings of the numbers, generally referred to as the *Nine Star Colors* assigns the following colors to the number 1 to 9, and further informs that it is the white colors that are regarded as the most auspicious *stars*. These white stars represent excellent intangible forces, and when occurring together bring fabulous good luck. By themselves the white stars enhance landscape feng shui features and are also effective in modifying any killing effects caused by inauspicious feng shui features or numbers.

The number 1 is white
The number 2 is black
The number 3 is pure green
The number 4 is light green
The number 5 is dull yellow
The number 6 is white
The number 7 is maroon or brown
The number 8 is white
The number 9 is purple

From the nine star color representations above, we observe the good luck numbers to be **1,6, and 8, w**hich confirms information given in texts dealing with the flying star school. The text further describes the black and yellow colors as inauspicious i.e. as represented by the numbers **2 and 5**. This too coincides with earlier research undertaken. The text further states that when black combines with yellow it represents extreme ill fortune. Therefore **2 with 5 is very bad.**

The **white stars** collectively are also known as the triple stars. When they occur together, they are deemed to bring extreme good fortune to the sector they occupy. Thus if in your period Lo-Shu you have the combination of 1,6 and 8 occurring in the sector that houses your main door or your bedroom, this portends extreme good fortune during the entire twenty year period for you. Furthermore, when the numbers 1,6 and 8 occur in that same sector under the annual/monthly movement of the Lo-Shu stars, then those are the month(s) when the predicted good fortune will very likely manifest itself.

THE AUSPICIOUS TRIPLES & DOUBLES

According to the texts there are certain numbers which when occurring as auspicious triples and doubles signify fabulous good fortune. The good fortune takes many forms - and does not always mean prosperity and wealth alone. According tot he Chinese, good fortune also mean having many sons, or having illustrious descendants who bring honor to the family name; it means being recognized and respected as an honorable man enjoying great prestige and power. The professions that represent good fortune are judges, ministers and generals, who in the old days personify the ruling elite of the country. Thus the meanings given should be read in the context of modern circumstances.

The TRIPLE 6's occurring in your significant sector means great wealth. Your children will be illustrious scholars. If you have three sons one of them will have a distinguished career in the army or the armed forces. If you have a triple 6 occurring in your period Lo-Shu, do try to *tap* it by either locating your study there or if this is not possible, try to have your bedroom located in that sector. Do not have your toilets and kitchen located in a sector with the triple 6 combination. This will have the effect of pressing on the good luck thereby dispersing it.

The TRIPLE 7 combination stress extremely good money luck during the current period This is because 7 is the ruling number of the present period. When you have a triple 7 (or even a double 7) again try to tap its excellent intangible forces by locating your important rooms here.

The DOUBLE 8 combination is particularly potent when it occurs in the South sector of your house. Such a house will produce powerful children who will bring prosperity and honor to the family name.

The DOUBLE 1 combination promises a brilliant generation and good luck is expected to continue for 60 years. Double 1's are very favorable when they occur in the North sector. Energize the double 1 with a water feature thereby tapping into the luck of the elements.

The DOUBLE 9 in the South is an extremely favorable combination. This is because the original Lo-Shu number of the South is also 9, and when a double 9 comes in, it really means there are three nines. This combination promises good fortune in the form of illustrious descendants and great prosperity for the entire household. Activate this good fortune further by having bright lights in the South.

Chapter Six
Wuxing - The Five Elements

Winds following one upon the other
The image of the gently penetrating,
Thus the superior man spreads his forces
And carries out his undertakings

From the I CHING on the
Hexagram Sun the Gentle

THE FIVE ELEMENTS

Much of the practice of feng shui involves understanding the significance of the five elements and their interactions with each other. These elements are FIRE, EARTH, WOOD, GOLD or METAL and WATER, and they have a **productive relationship** as well as a **destructive relationship** with each other. The diagnosis of "good" or "bad" flying star feng shui has much to do with interpreting the meanings and symbolism of these elements, as indicated by the numbers, as well as their relationships with each other.

According to the Chinese Calendar - the Ganzhi system of time measurement and classifications - auspicious and inauspicious events in the universe depend upon interactions between the heavenly stems and twelve *earthly branches.*

The heavenly stems comprise of the five elements - each with a yang (positive) or yin (negative) nature. Because the elements are viewed as manifestations of heaven's luck on earthly events, the importance of interpreting the meanings of the elements in feng shui cannot be over stressed. The stems are potent indicators!

The earthly branches meanwhile refer to the twelve animals of the Chinese zodiac, and in the Chinese fortune telling, both the stems and the branches feature in any divination reading. Thus, for example, when one investigates one's destiny based on one's date of birth, according to the Ganzhi system, one discovers that each lunar year is symbolized by an animal (the earthly branch) as well as by an element either positive or negative in nature (the heavenly stem).

From this relationship alone, the fortune teller is able to offer general readings of characteristics, affinities and so forth. And in these readings the element relationship is vital to an accurate forecast.

Those who consult fortunetellers for in depth investigation of their fortunes will also become familiar with their *eight characters.* These characters are based on their **four pillars of destiny** i.e. their year , month, day and hour of birth.

CHAPTER
SIX

The
Five
Elements

The EIGHT
Characters

| Wuxing - the Five Elements | **Six** |

THE EIGHT CHARACTERS or Paht Chee

Each of the eight characters symbolize one of the five elements. Many Chinese believe that the reading of one's destiny under this system offers the most authentic and accurate prediction of what destiny holds in store for any individual. Naturally the accuracy of the prediction depends on how well the fortune teller has interpreted and diagnosed the inter relationship between these elements.

In making his reading, the fortune teller goes deep into element analysis - studying the five different symbols for subtle nuances that add vital clues to the interactions that cause impending good or bad fortunes. And because every "*pillar*" of the Chinese calendar - hour, day, month and year - is also represented by these same five elements, analyzing their various and changing relationships presents something of a major challenge. The "secrets" of one's destiny stay locked if, as a result of the complexities of analyses, the fortuneteller makes a wrong interpretation. Deciphering the meanings of element relationships is far from easy, and the difference between a good fortuneteller and a not so good one is how skillful they are at interpreting the affiliations of these elements.

The same is true in the practice of feng shui.

Element analysis feature strongly in every school of feng shui.

Irrespective of the method of computation used, the feng shui practitioner MUST first of all be able to "identify" each and every object encountered in terms of the five elements. And after that, to decipher the meanings attached to them as the *interact* with each other.

THE ELEMENTS in FLYING STAR

In Flying Star feng shui, element analysis is vital to its successful practice. To start with, each of the numbers **1** to **9** has a corresponding element. And irrespective of where the numbers *fly* to, their original element symbol remains the same.

For instance, **the number 9** signifies the **element *fire*** and if in the flow of it's "flight" around the Lo Shu, the number 9 lands in the east, then we know that 9 has entered wood, that fire has entered wood which could well pose a danger for wood ! This is because East symbolizes wood. A situation where *fire has entered wood* is good for the fire but it exhausts the wood, the host location. Thus fire coming into the East is not good for the East. This reflects the relationship between fire and wood.

Now, according to the relationship cycles, we know that wood feeds the fire. Why? Because wood produces fire . Thus wood is good for fire. But in this case wood did not come to fire. It was fire which came into wood. And we know that fire burns wood.

In such a situation, it would appear that the effect of fire coming into wood is less than auspicious! Fire coming into wood cannot be good for the wood! It cannot be good for the sector symbolized … in this case the sector east.

Another example. Suppose the **number 6 flies into the south**. What is the interpretation? The number 6 is metal or gold. When it flies into the south it is flying into fire. This is because the element of the south is fire. We know from the cycle of relationships that fire destroys metal; thus fire is more powerful than metal.

So when metal comes into fire, it has no power to harm the fire, unlike the previous example where the incoming element has the power to hit the sitting element. In this particular example therefore, 6 coming into south does not have any bad effects.

If this were all there was to element analysis, things would be very simple indeed.

CHAPTER
SIX

The
Five
Elements

The
ELEMENTS
in
Flying Star

Wuxing – the Five Elements	**Six**

In flying star we must consider the effect of all the numbers inside each of the sector, or grids. There are initially three numbers inside the natal chart of a dwelling place. These are the main star numerals, the chor sin and the siang sin numerals.

It is necessary to analyze the interaction between these three numbers. Because this can be a very complex and tedious exercise for the casual practitioner, we have extracted and summarized the "meanings" of combinations of numbers elsewhere in this book from old Chinese feng shui text on numerology. This makes the exercise of interpretation a little easier to understand.

For those who wish to undertake their own detailed investigations and have their own interpretations of the element perspective, just remember the key to correct interpretation. This is to examine the relationship of each of the secondary star numerals with the main numerals first before examining the relationship of the secondary stars with each other.

Start by making sure you fully understand the elements and what they symbolize and/or are symbolized by. Thus to summarize briefly:

The element FIRE is red, anything bright anything shiny anything that gives out light. Fire is also symbolized by summer, by heat, by lighting and by warmth. Fire is also symbolized by the sun and by sunshine. In the Pa Kua, fire in south, the phoenix and the middle daughter

The element WATER is blue or black, anything liquid - rivers, lakes, fountains, waterfalls, the sea, ponds, aquariums and all other objects that simulate the flow of water. In the Pa Kua, water is north, the turtle and the middle son. In terms of seasons, water corresponds to winter.

The element Wood is green, any kind of plant life - trees, shrubs, flowers, grass, and all objects that are made of wood, like furniture - tables and chairs, cupboards and shelves, carve ornamentals and so forth. In the Pa Kua, two directions, the southeast (small wood) and the east (big wood), represent wood. The east also symbolizes the green dragon, thunder and the eldest son; while the south east represents the wind and the eldest daughter.

The element **METAL or GOLD** is white or metallic, any kind of object made from metal and steel, gold or silver - like trains and cars, ships and airplanes. Gold jewelry also symbolizes this element, so that for those lacking or needing to expand the presence of metal in their life, wearing gold is recommended. In the Pa Kua, the northwest, which also symbolizes the father and heaven represents big metal; while the west, which stands for the youngest daughter, is small metal.

And finally, the element EARTH is brown or yellow, any kind of object which comes from the ground and is not metal e.g. boulders and stones, pebbles, natural quartz crystals, a replica of the globe. In the Pa Kua the southwest and the northeast both symbolize earth. The southwest is the big earth because this is the direction, which symbolizes the matriarch or earth mother. The northeast is also the mountain and the youngest son.

From the above list of symbolic representations, the astute practitioner can start to analyze the feng shui elemental "characteristics" or "attributes" of the various corners of his/her house or office, and in so doing, begin to enhance these corners after studying the relationship cycles. Another approach is to investigate the element characteristics of the corner which houses your bedroom, and from thereon undertake to amplify it's element luck thereby improving your feng shui.

THE RELATIONSHIP CYCLES OF THE FIVE ELEMENTS

THE PRODUCTIVE CYCLE

WOOD produces FIRE produces EARTH produces METAL produces WATER produces WOOD and so on

THE DESTUCTIVE CYCLE

WOOD destroys EARTH destroys WATER destroys FIRE destroys METAL destroys WOOD and so on

113

CHAPTER
SIX

The
Five
Elements

The
ELEMENTS
in
Flying Star

Wuxing - the Five Elements | **Six**

As you progress deeper into the practice of feng shui, (and for those of you who consult feng shui masters) you should become aware of the fact that a great deal of feng shui *cures, enhances and interpretations* have to do with the simulation and manipulation of the five *elements* within the environment. Understand this basic principle and you will have understood one of the fundamental explanations of feng shui.

The complexity of feng shui practice arises from the fact that according to the Chinese ancient manuals, everything in the world, indeed, in the universe, can be classified as one of these five elements.

<u>**Symbolically therefore**</u>, every object and structure has an elemental relationship with each other! **Colors** symbolize the elements. **Names** symbolize elements. **Years,** months periods, hours symbolize elements. **Animals** symbolize elements. Indeed, the five elements embrace, and are constituents of everything that exists in the universe, and accordingly, are believed to exert powerful yet intangible abstract forces on events as well as on the outcomes of events. The forces of the elements that surround his world influence man's daily life, his fortunes and his destiny.

The good news is that these elements may be manipulated in a way which ensures there is harmony and balance. Successfully doing this is what good feng shui practice is all about! Thereby ensuring that any all of the intangible forces created are moving in a highly auspicious manner bringing harmonious forces to those whose lives are affected.

EXAMPLES:
In the Chinese pantheon, **lion is metal, tiger is earth**. Chair is wood. A red carpet is fire. Blue is water and plants are wood ...and so on.

<u>Thus:</u>
If your front door is threatened by fierce looking protective lions from the house across the road, you cannot fight these lions with tigers. Why? Because lions are metal and tigers are earth. The lion's metal energy will exhaust the tiger's earth energy. This is because earth produce metal and this means metal exhausts earth! The way to fight the lions is to use the element fire, which destroys metal. Thus hanging a red banner across the front door will overcome the fierce shar chi of the lions across the road

THE LATER HEAVEN PA KUA & THE ELEMENTS

When analyzing the elements, refer to the simplified Pa Kua of symbols illustrated here for valuable insights into interpretations.

Note the Trigrams in each of the compass sectors and note also the direction indicated in the outermost ring. Studying the Pa Kua enables you to gain deeper insights into the Elements.

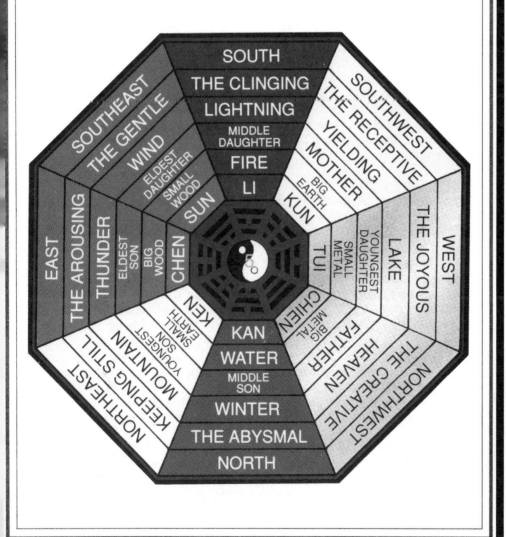

CHAPTER
SIX

The
Five
Elements

Reading the
ELEMENTS

Wuxing - the Five Elements	**Six**

ADDITIONAL LESSONS

EXAMPLE
If the **East sector** is adversely affected by bad luck numbers **2**(earth) and **5** (earth) flying in to cause problems, the effect is modified by the fact that East represents wood. According to the cycle of the elements *wood destroys earth*! Thus the ill effects of 2 and 5 are not as severe here in this East sector as it would be in say, the North which is symbolized by the element of water. This is because earth destroys water. Thus if the North of your house has the 2/5 combination the luck is exceedingly bad for whoever is there.

ANOTHER EXAMPLE:
If the **West sector** (small metal) is occupied by the auspicious numbers **1** (water); **6**(big metal) and **8**(small earth) the result is good for the sector because the big metal of 6 enhances or strengthens the west sector's small metal. Meanwhile the earth of **8** producers more metal. The combination is thus harmonious and extremely lucky for whoever is occupying that corner of the house. If that corner is a public place like a dining room then everyone benefits.

METAL ON WOOD
Take cognizance of whether the element being represented is large or small. Thus the effect of big metal on wood and small metal on wood is totally different. Big metal on big wood could be tractors and chain saws cutting down a forest of trees - symbolizing destruction, not a good sign at all! On the other hand, small metal could be on small wood could be an implement turning the wood into furniture - symbolizing prediction, a good sign! Metal on wood can be bad or good therefore, depending on the nature of the object symbolized and if it involves any of the symbols of the Pa Kua. We have to see whether we are dealing with big or small versions of the elements!

THE DANGER OF EARTH
Of the five elements, earth often signifies misfortune, and earth is symbolized by the southwest, the northeast and the center. Earth is very yin, and too much of it symbolizes the power of darkness, death and cold. It must be overcome by yang - i.e. fire, brightness and growth.

But **only one direction signifies fire, and that is the south**. It is for this reason that the south is regarded as such an auspicious direction by many schools of feng shui. In flying Star therefore the sector South is often regarded as the strongest sector as it has the best potential to dominate the deadly earth numerals of 5 and 2.

WOOD and FIRE

Wood is the element that signifies growth. Wood is represented by the sector East (big wood) and the Southeast (small wood). The color green represents wood. In the East the green is the pure translucent variety. This is represented by the number **3**. In the South east the green is light in color and is represented by the number **4**.

The wood element is regarded as the most powerful symbol of growth. According to the stages of life wood represents youth. And in the seasons, wood represents spring. In the spring, wood reigns supreme. And in the summer it is in full bloom - a time for harvesting.

In the winter however, wood is weak. It feels the cold. It hibernates. The leaves of plants drop off. It requires the warmth of the sun. It requires fire to keep it insulated from the cold. Thus **when a combination of wood numbers come onto a wood sector during the spring and summer, the indication is good feng shui. But if it happens during the winter it is not as auspicious.** Fire coming into wood during the winter is regarded as strengthening rather than destructive, even though wood is said to feed the fire. Thus there are occasions when general guidelines need to be tempered by other considerations.

GENERAL GUIDELINES

General guidelines say that wood is produced by water, and that it in turn feeds the fire. It is thus exhausted by fire. Wood is destroyed by metal, but as we have seen earlier, this destruction interpretation must also be tampered by other considerations and finally, wood destroys earth, as the roots of the plant dig deep into the soil exhausting it of its nourishment.

Knowing these varied and multiple characteristics enables the practitioner to understand the deeper implication of the numbers, because we shall see later, each of the numbers 1 to 9 also represent one of the five elements As they fly around the Lo Shu grid, their meanings are transformed by the influence of the elements. The elements and their corresponding numbers are summarized in this Table.

NUMBER	ELEMENT	NUMBER	ELEMENT
1	WATER	6	BIG METAL
2	BIG EARTH	7	SMALL METAL
3	BIG WOOD	8	SMALL EARTH
4	SMALL WOOD	9	FIRE
5	MEDIUM EARTH		

CHAPTER
SIX

The
Five
Elements

The
NUMBERS
and the
ELEMENTS

Wuxing – the Five Elements	**Six**

THE NUMBERS AND THE ELEMENTS

We see therefore that analysis of flying star numbers extends beyond the meanings of numbers and combinations of the numbers. The practitioner must consider the symbolic elements attached to each of the numbers. Thus, under the Later Heaven Pa Kua arrangement of numbers 1 to 9 have the following relationships.

- Number 1 is WATER
- Number 2 is BIG EARTH
- Number 3 is BIG WOOD
- Number 4 is SMALL WOOD
- Number 5 is MEDIUM EARTH
- Number 6 is BIG METAL
- Number 7 is SMALL METAL
- Number 8 is SMALL EARTH
- Number 9 is FIRE

In Flying Star method, element analysis of the numbers based on the "relationships of the elements to each other " is extremely useful when attempting to diagnose the good and bad luck months if each year. The analysis becomes more intense when the respective month and year "*star numbers*" are compared and/or combined with the star numbers of the natal chart.

To simplify the analysis, initially study only the numbers in the important sectors of your house i.e. those sectors which have a direct bearing on your own well-being and luck for a particular period, year or month.

In a residential house, the important sectors are where the main door, the master bedroom or other important (i.e. frequently used) rooms are located.

If you wish to examine the luck of the house for a particular individual, first determine which sector of the house she/he lives in and then analyze the numbers in that relevant sectors. Usually this means the bedroom or a study frequently used by the person.

When you analyze the nature of the element relationships, remember that while the numbers "fly" around the Lo Shu grid, their <u>element</u> symbolism does not change irrespective of the direction/location they have flown to.

Elemental and number relationships are widely used by Masters when analyzing monthly and annual feng shui luck of buildings and houses. The practice is particularly widespread in Hong Kong where the flying star method is popular. Summarized below are some of the meanings and relationships of numbers, which can be used for monthly/annual feng shui checkups.

MONTHLY/ANNUAL ANALYSIS OF NUMBERS.

Feng Shui Masters usually work out the numbers of each of the twelve months of the year when attempting to predict the fortune for the following year. This is done in exactly the same way that the twelve monthly Lo Shu's were calculated earlier on in Chapter Four for the twelve lunar months if the lunar years 1999 to 2001.

These monthly Lo Shu's are presented every year in the Annual Tong Shu. With the 12 monthly Lo Shu's ascertained, you can start your analysis by drawing up another grid – this time to spotlight the number (and element) which flies in each month, and which reacts with the year number in all of the nine sectors of the grid.

Example:

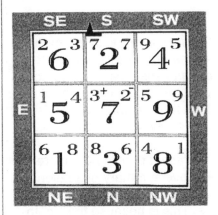

A lucky natal chart but 1999 will not be a good year for this house

Let us say your house was built in the Period of 7 and its main door is located in the South and facing the 1st subsection direction of the South. The natal chart of the house is as shown here (**also in Page 49**) . Now you wish to investigate what the luck of your house will be like, in the year 1999, when your husband is due for an important promotion. What you do is you now turn to **Pages 79 to 81 to study the 12 monthly charts of 1999**. Already you know you have the double 7 in the South, which is excellent. <u>But from the monthly charts you note that the SOUTH has the awful 5 and is afflicted</u>. It is unlikely your husband will get that promotion in 1999.

CHAPTER
SIX

The
Five
Elements

Monthly &
Annual
analysis

Wuxing - the Five Elements | **Six**

Example:

Still on the same house which has its front door in the South -One ...

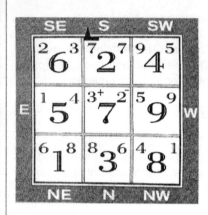

We have noted that in 1999 the front door of this house being in the South is afflicted by the *wu wang* or **5** yellow. It is recommended that another door be used throughout the year . The 5 Yellow configuration is much feared as it affects 45 degrees of the compass. It brings illness and loss. The best way to overcome it is to use a five rod windchime. Hang it in front of the main door to allow for the metal to exhaust the afflicted earth of 5. Otherwise 1999 will be a very difficult year for the residents of this house. The worst month is 8th Sept to 8th October.

The effect of the Seasons

There is also a method of analysis that is based on the significance of the seasons. Remember that monthly cycles of time reflect the cycle of the seasons. Thus during the first three months of Spring, the earth power of feng shui is very positive and strong and everything is just starting to grow. In some years e.g. the year 2001, there are two springs (two Lap Chuns).

Such years are generally regarded as auspicious years. In the months of summer, fire energy dominates. It is a time of harvests and much celebration. There is a preponderance of *yang* essence. Next comes Autumn, when saving up for the winter becomes the order of the day. And finally there is winter when everything stops growing. Winter is cold and very *yin*. There is a shortage of heat and an excess of water.

Analysis of the numbers and what they represent should not ignore the effects of Nature's cycles. Based on the above summary of seasonal attributes we can go deeper in our analysis of the luck of the above house based on the SOUTH sector alone. This is because the South sector is where the main door is located, and anything that affects the main door has the most vital bearing and importance on the luck of the house.

Example: **... the reading confirms that 1999 is a bad year for the main door sector of this same house**

Spring: (first lunar month of 1999 – see page 79) **# 3 into # 5**
When the (month) number 3 "flies" into the (year) number 5, it means big wood has flown into medium earth. We have to investigate the effect of wood on earth to note the effects for that month. We note that wood can grow in earth, so the effect is "good" but it can be made even better if we place some water in the sector, because then, the wood will grow even faster ! Plus it is Spring, a time of fast growth- so this is a doubly auspicious time for wood to have come into the south because it is a time of growth. Also because the earth here is the inauspicious 5 it is excellent that the wood that has come in is big wood. This enables it to overcome the earth. Interpretation? The wood is controlling the bad 5 to some extent.

SPRING: (second lunar month of 1999 – see page 79) **# 2 into # 5**
Here we have a very dangerous combination. Big earth coming into medium earth in a sector of fire causes too much earth. The house is weighted down with extreme bad luck. Occurring in Spring it is doubly unlucky. The sector badly needs water, both to put out the fire and to contain the earth. Thus between 18th March to 15th April, anyone living in a house with the main door facing South first subsection will need to be very very careful.

SPRING: (Third lunar month of 1999 – see page 79) **# 1 into # 5**
The combination indicates water coming into earth in a sector of fire. Place a strong plant in the sector to tap the ingredients of growth that can lead to a good harvest. This is because the time is Spring, a time of strong growth. But also be careful . From an element perspective, 1 represents water, and water is supposed to be destroyed by earth so the year number 5 overcomes the month number 1. Because the year number is inauspicious, the indication for the third month is to continue to be careful.

SUMMER (fourth lunar month – see page 79)**# 9 into # 5**
Fire comes into earth. As we know, fire produces earth. Thus fire flying in magnifies the power of the bad 5. It produces more of the element that feeds the unlucky 5. Plus, it is summer which enhances fire. Very inauspicious.

SUMMER (fifth lunar month – see page 80)**# 8 into # 5**
The effect of 8 into 5 is metal coming into earth. Metal exhausts earth and in this case it is good because this means the troublesome 5 is under control. Because it is summer however the power of metal is weak since the fire of summer overcomes metal.

CHAPTER
SIX

The
Five
Elements

Seasonal
Analysis

Wuxing - the Five Elements | **Six**

Example: **... continuing the monthly and seasonal reading for 1999 for the main door sector of the same house**

Summer: (sixth lunar month – see page 80) **# 7 into # 5**
When 7 comes into the south, small metal is flying into the earth in a fire sector. The metal exhausts the earth 5 thereby ensuring that for this month at least the effect of the 5 has been dampened somewhat. But is summer and earth is in plentiful supply. The sector continues to have bad luck. Residents continue to have problems with court cases and other nasty inconveniences.

Autumn (Seventh lunar month – see page 80) **# 6 into # 5**
6 and 5 means big metal into earth. This month will see some respite from the bad luck of 5. Also because it is Autumn, the power of fire has waned somewhat and big metal will exhaust the earth. The influence of the 5 is reducing...

Autumn (Eighth lunar month – see page 80) **# 5 into # 5**
The pernicious double 5 brings bad breath, ill health and very severe bad luck during the month. Residents of this house will fall sick this month or could even succumb to an accident if the natal chart stars indicate 5 here. It is a good thing that there are double 7s here in the natal chart. This can serve as a counter to the combination of deadly stars. However there is a 2 in the main star numeral causing the bad luck brought by the double 5 to become compounded. Be very careful this month. Stay quiet and lie low. Do not take risks and do not launch any business or new venture.

The foregoing example of analysis will have given you the method and rationale behind monthly and seasonal investigation of the numbers based on Wuxing or five elements. Remember that the element in the months between the seasons is deemed to be months when the earth element is strong. Remember also that the unluckiest numbers in flying star feng shui are 5 and 2 both of which numbers belong to the earth element. Thus it is advisable for you to structure your element analysis around the attributes of the earth element.

Another useful tip to remember is to always start your analysis with the sector where the door is located. This is the most significant sector in terms of anything being outstandingly good or being outstandingly bad in any year. Remember that a even if you have an excellent natal chart, as in the case of the example above, you can still succumb to deadly flying stars and need to take care.

That which is bright rises twice ...

That which is
bright rises
twice,
The image
of fire. The
superior man
perpetuates
his brightness
and
illuminates the
four corners of
the world.

**From the I
CHING on the
Hexagram Li**

Chapter Seven
Flying Star Case Studies

At the foot of the mountain is water providing nourishment. The superior man is generous with his food and careful with his words...

From the I CHING on the Hexagram I – Providing Nourishment

Flying Star Case Studies

The cases featured here are to enable readers get a better feel for the various applications of Flying Star Feng Shui. These Cases demonstrate the method of drawing up the relevant Lo Shu grids for analyses and offer insights into interpretive questions.

Some of the examples given also suggest how practitioners can defer or speed up plans for renovations, for expanding businesses, for making a career change and so forth. By obtaining indications on the suitability of the time They will be able to decide better ie on whether to proceed or to wait for a more auspicious time. In such cases, indications of feng shui at home can also be supplemented with a reading of the time aspect of feng shui at the office.

The cases highlighted in this chapter deal only with time aspects of feng shui, and do not take into account other compass or landscape feng shui considerations. In the practice of feng shui however, these other spatial concepts of feng shui cannot be ignored. They MUST be factored into any feng shui analysis of a house or building to ensure that the picture which emerges is as complete as possible.

Shown here is a very auspicious painting of **Fuk Luk Sau** the three star Gods of Health. Wealth and Prosperity. Display them in your home to help you overcome bad flying stars ...

CHAPTER
SEVEN

Flying
Star
Case
Studies

CASE
ONE

Flying Star Case Studies	**Seven**

CASE ONE

To investigate the auspicious and inauspicious sectors of this link house during the period of 7 (1984 to 2003)... and to analyze feng shui luck of the house during the year 1999.

FEATURES OF THE HOUSE

The house was actually built in 1990, so the Lo Shu natal chart of the house is based on the period of 7. The <u>main door of the house faces North</u> and it is located in the sub sector nearest the East i.e. the <u>third sub sector of the north</u> sector. The back of the house is deemed to be in the south sector.

COMPUTATION OF THE RELEVANT LO SHU GRID
see also page 48

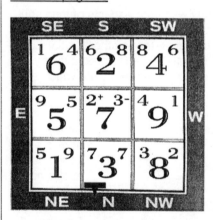

The Lo Shu grid, as shown here has 7 as the reigning number. So 7 goes into the center. The siang sin star in the center is 3 because the back front door is in the north, and the chor sin star is 2, because back door is deemed to be in the south directly opposite the front door.

The flight of the siang sin is minus (-) because it's center number is odd, and the flight of the chor sin is plus (+) because its center number is even.

INITIAL ANALYSIS

- This house enjoys excellent feng shui during the 20 year period being investigated because of the "double 7" combination of the secondary stars in the north sector, where the main door is located. This is an indication of auspicious feng shui.

- North symbolizes the water element. The main star number is 3. It symbolizes wood. According to the manuals, water produces wood enabling it to grow brilliantly. But in this case it is wood that has flown into water, thereby exhausting the water. So the excellent fortune indicated by the double 7 is somewhat curbed by the exhaustive nature of the combination of elements.

CASE ONE contd …

- The other auspicious sectors in the house are the **South** (with **6 & 8**); and the **Southwest** (with **8 & 6**); so its best if the main bedrooms are located in either of these sectors. The Southeast and West are neutral while the East and Northeast are unlucky because these sectors house the **5s**. The center of the house should be kept as silent as possible to reduce friction and quarrels because of the **2 & 3** combination.

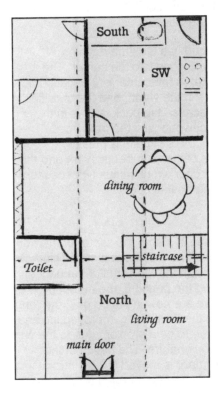
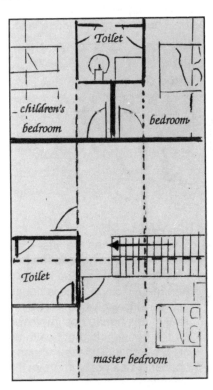

Shown above are the floor plans of the house. It has two levels so the rooms on both levels should be examined based on the initial reading of the Lo Shu numbers. **The main door is auspicious**. Above it is the master bedroom upstairs - and having this important room here is good. However, the master bedroom also falls in the Northwest sector which houses the 2 and 3 quarrelsome combination. So residents sleeping in this room must guard against having too much noise here. There should be no radio or TV kept in the master bedroom. Let the NW sector be as quiet as possible. Otherwise there will be a great deal of unpleasantness and quarreling.

CHAPTER
SEVEN

Flying
Star
Case
Studies

CASE
TWO

Flying Star Case Studies

Seven

CASE TWO ...
To investigate the feng shui of a mansion constructed in the **period of 6** (1964 - 1983), and to analyze the luck of the house during year 1999.

FEATURES OF THE HOUSE
This mansion was built in 1970. The natal chart of the house is indicated in the Lo Shu below. The main door of this house also faces North, and is located exactly in the middle sector; thus the sub sector is the second sub sector. The back of the house is located in the South.

North

The basic grid has 6 as the reigning number. So 6 goes into the center. The siang sin star in the center is 2 because the front door is in the North, and the chor sin star is 1, because the back door is in the south, directly opposite the front door. The flight of the siang sin is plus (+) because its center number is even, and the flight of the chor sin us minus (-) because its center number is odd.

INITIAL ANALYSIS
- This mansion has the auspicious 7 siang sin star in the sector of the front door. But it also houses the inauspicious **5** as the chor sin star. This indicates that when the house was first built the feng shui of the house was inauspicious. This is because during the period 6, the number 7 was deemed inauspicious. However since we are now in period of 7, the feng shui of this house has improved. In fact the 7 will bring improved income for the household; but health will continue to be a problem due to the chor sin 5 which indicates sickness of a serious nature. The health of the household can only improve if the main door is moved OR by introducing "renovations" thereby changing the natal chart (to a period of 7 house). This is a major exercise requiring consideration.
- Another feature of the front door sector is the main numeral is 2, and when combined with 5, this is another indicator of ill health, and sickness. This combination can also cause fatal accidents for the residents.
- The 7/5 combination of secondary stars is repeated in the Northeast sector . This is the location of the master bedroom upstairs. Again the 7 brings good luck but the 5 brings illness. This house has a bathroom placed directly above the front door. Usually this "presses" down on any good luck coming into the house and here it presses down on the 7. But in so doing it is also pressing down the unlucky 5 !

CASE TWO ….contd.

THE LUCK OF THE HOUSE DURING 1999

To Investigate the feng shui luck of the house during the twelve months of 1999, we need to refer to the Lo Shu of 1999 which has 1 in the center as the reigning number of the year. Please refer to pages 79 to 81 for the Lo Shu grids of all twelve months of 1999 as they interact with the year number. *By checking how the monthly numbers combine with the year number for the North sector which houses the front door we can obtain a "reading" for the luck of this mansion.*

Based on the year Lo Shu, the house is headed for a good year in 1999 especially for the Patriarch or breadwinner of the house. This is because the main star numeral in the North where the door is located is a 6. This is an auspicious number that benefits the head of the house. Also 6 is metal coming into a water sector enhances water. It is an excellent indication. The best months are fourth, sixth, seventh and eighth months of the year.

In 1999 the sector to watch out for is the **South** because this is the location of the **Five yellows**. The bad luck of the 5 is felt hardest of all in the eight month when a double 5 configuration is observed (see page 80). In this house the South is probably occupied by the back door and the kitchen. If this is the case the kitchen will press down on the Five yellows. For good measure you can also hang a five rod windchime to control the effect of the bad fives.

If you observe the Lo Shu natal chart above however you will note that the back sector of South has the double 6 which is very auspicious. This lucky double is however afflicted in 1999 otherwise the Patriarch of the house will enjoy fantastic income luck. In any case the double 6 has been weakened by the element of fire in the South sector.

Finally according to the natal chart you will note that the 2/5 combination occupies the Southeast. This spells danger for anyone staying in that sector. Illness and accidents are indicated and in the year 1999, the months to be very wary of are the third month (16th April to 14th May); the sixth month (13th July to 10th August) and the twelfth month (7th Jan to 4th Feb).

Readers will note from the above analysis that if you want to you can actually pinpoint the exact dates when dangerous flying stars can cause problems related to loss and ill health and accidents.

CHAPTER
SEVEN

Flying
Star
Case
Studies

CASE
THREE

Flying Star Case Studies

CASE THREE
When Mrs. Jegaratnam was appointed the director at a college in Subang Jaya, she had been given the corner room of a third floor general office and wished to investigate whether the feng shui of her office would be good for her during 1994 and 1995. She wished to know if she would be happy at her new job.

FEATURES OF THE OFFICE
The layout plan of the third floor general office together with its natal chart are reproduced in the sketch below. Mrs. Jega's room is in the Northwest corner of the floor. In relation to the main entrance, her room enjoys relatively good feng shui. Because she is a west group person, the NW is a favorable sector for her. But her sitting direction facing east is not so favorable.

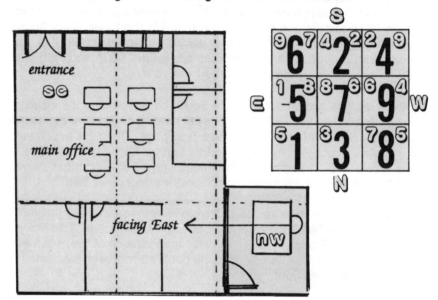

Because the building of this college was completed in 1986, it's reigning Lo Shu number is 7. The siang sin star in the center is 6 and the chor sin star is 8. As the main entrance is in the first sub sector of SE, the flying mode for both star is minus.

From the natal chart I was able to give Mrs. Jega a reading of her feng shui luck for the remainder of this twenty year period i.e. up to 2003. I could also work out the feng shui luck of the office over the next two years by drawing up the annual and monthly Lo Shu charts of the office. Let us walk through the flying star feng shui of Mrs Jega's office.

CASE THREE contd …

THE ANALYSIS of MRS JEGA'S OFFICE

Mrs Jega's office natal chart is the one on Page 57. Mrs. Jega's room is located in the **Northwest corner** of the office floor. The NW enjoys the auspicious number **8,** and this is supplemented by the chor sin star of **7**, both of which are good fortune indicators. These numerals in this corner indicate financial success for Mrs Jega from her job.

However the **siang sin star numeral is the unlucky 5,** which indicates problems relating to health. The effect of the pernicious 5 is to cause periodic illness for the occupant. The way to "press" down on the 5 is to use a 5 rod wind chime. Hanging a wind chime in her office will assist Mrs. Jega stay healthy, and not succumb to sickness frequently.

It is also useful to examine the location of the entrance to the office. This is the **Southeast sector** of the floor where the combination of numbers are **6, 7 and 9** all of which are auspicious. This brings general good luck to all the occupants on the floor. The feng shui is thus said to be good.

The annual 1994 Lo Shu which had 6 in the center, and the auspicious 7 in Mrs. Jega's NW corner brought good fortune for Mrs Jega. She enjoyed excellent months in the $6^{th}/7^{th}/8^{th}/10^{th}$ months i.e. up to 7th December. In 1995, the annual Lo Shu number changed to reigning number 5 in the center. This brought the auspicious **6** to Mrs. Jega's **NW** corner - again she enjoyed good luck in 1995.

It was clear from the Lo Shu grids that Mrs. Jega should derive good feng shui luck from the office throughout most of 1994 and 1995. And indeed she did enjoy excellent upward mobility in her career with the College all through the years 1994 and 1995.

In 1996 however, problems started. This was because in 1996, the pernicious annual Lo Shu **5 flew** into Mrs Jega's **NW** sector. In that year whenever this **5** combined with **2** or with **5** itself, severe problems plagued Mrs. Jega. As it turned out Mrs Jega constantly fell ill during 1996. At work she fell out with the new College Principal and by the middle of the year she had submitted her resignation. It was to be lucky she left when she did. **Her successor occupied her old office and sad to say met with a fatal car accident in the eighth month of the year. That month the stars in that NW office were 2 and 5… Coincidence or feng shui ?**

CHAPTER
SEVEN

Flying
Star
Case
Studies

CASE
FOUR

Flying Star Case Studies

CASE FOUR

Mr. & Mrs. Teng were about to purchase a new house located in a township development near Ampang. They wished to investigate its feng shui over the next twenty years. House and main door directions had already been ascertained to be very auspicious for Mr. Teng.

FEATURES OF THE HOUSE

The layout plans of the house are reproduced on the facing page. Mr. Teng is about to finalize the S&P agreement. The main door of the house faces north. But it is located in the third sub sector of the Northwest corner of the house. **North** is Mr. Teng's best direction under the Pa Kua Lo Shu compass school method of identifying auspicious directions, The main door direction is thus ideal for Mr. Teng. Landscape wise, the house also enjoys good feng shui. All that's left is to investigate the time dimension.

COMPUTATION OF THE LO SHU NATAL CHART

This is a Period 7 house as it has only recently been completed. Its main door is placed in the third sub sector of the **Northwest location**.

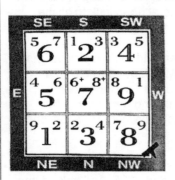

So the center number of the **siang sin star is 8** and the **chor sin star is 6**. Both these stars fly in a plus mode as they are both even numbers and the door is located in the third sub sector (of North). The natal chart is shown here on the left. Note the numbers in the **NW** which is where the door is located.

INITIAL ANALYSIS

Based on the natal chart it is possible to investigate the house luck for the Period of 7 which lasts until 2003. The main door numbers in the NW sector indicate both current and future prosperity for the residents. (The three numbers **7,8 and 9** are very auspicious numbers). The SE of the house has a chor sin 5 and the SW has a siang sin 5. The back half of the house is not as lucky as the front half of the house. The best location for the master bedroom is in the center or in the West sector of the house. I told Mr. Teng way back then that although he is an EAST group person Mr. Teng should **not** sleep in the North or the South sector of the house because these two sectors house the deadly **2/3** combination. If the master bedroom is located in either of these sectors, husband and wife will be sure to split !

CASE FIVE

In mid July of 1994, Mrs. Lau's entire family fell ill, and her aged father who lived with her, succumbed to a heart attack. In early October her eldest son had a serious, almost fatal accident. I investigated the time dimension feng shui of her house to see if it had anything to do with the bad luck suffered by Mrs. Lau in that year.

FEATURES OF MRS. LAU'S HOUSE

The house is nearly 30 years old having been **built in 1965**, during **the Period of 6.** It's natal chart thus has a 6 in the center. The main door is located in the NORTH sector, which is circled for ease of reference. This chart with its chor sin and siang sin stars is reproduced below. Readers will notice that 1994 also has 6 as the ruling Lo Shu number. **The Natal Chart of the house is on the left and the Chart for Oct/Nov 1994 is on the right.**

LO Shu stars for 9th month 1994

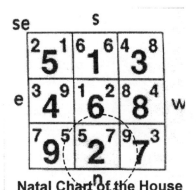

Natal Chart of the House

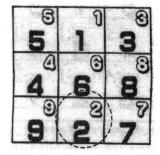

Note that in the 9th month of 1994 the main door in the North is very badly hit by the double 2. This seriously compounded the deadly 5/2 combination in the main door sector of the natal thereby causing the accident for the son in the month of October.

From monthly grid chart shown above please also note another bad luck combination ie the double 5 in the SE where as it happened Mrs Lau's father had his bedroom. Note also the repeat 2/5 combination also in the SE sector of the natal chart.

It is no wonder that Mrs Lau's father succumbed to the heart attack in August. His bedroom suffered from a double whammy in the form of the bad luck 5 appearing in both the natal chart and the 1994 annual chart. To combat the pernicious 5 and 2, Mrs. Lau must hang a wind chime in both the north and southeast sectors.

CHAPTER
SEVEN

Flying
Star
Case
Studies

CASE
SIX

CASE SIX

Jerry and Mazlan, two young Malaysians recently graduated from university in the United States decided to open a cowboy theme restaurant catering to the affluent yuppies of K.L. Jerry's wife Janice decided to consult her mother's long time friend Mr. Yap who was most knowledgeable about feng shui. After several sessions, the plans for the restaurant opened for business early in the year and business has been steadily building up. Let us see if the restaurant's good business can sustain.

LAYOUT PLAN OF THE RESTAURANT

Below is the layout plan of the new restaurant; which has been scrutinized previously by the feng shui master. The directions of the doors and tables have been laid out to match the most auspicious directions of the owners. Now all that's left to do is check the flying star feng shui.

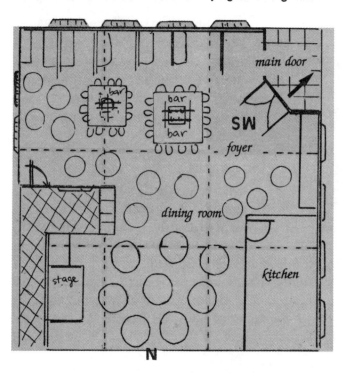

Note: The entrance is facing southwest to match the partners auspicious direction. This was based on the Pa Kua Lo Shu formula of Directions. To see if the restaurant's business can sustain over a period of time we have to use the Flying Star formula.

Shown on the next page is the natal chart of the restaurant. The flights of the siang sin (- mode) and chor sin (+ mode) stars have been worked out according to the flying star formula. The door here is deemed to be in the second sub sector of the SW corner. The Lo Shu is Period of 7.

CASE SIX contd ...

The natal chart (shown below) indicates extremely good luck for the restaurant throughout the period of 7 i.e. up till the year 2003. This is because of the **double 7 star combination occurring in the SW** - the sector of the main entrance. This means that the overall flying star luck for the restaurant is excellent for this reigning period of 7.

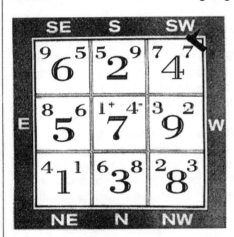

I investigated the "luck" of the restaurant for 1994 and 1995 to see if the overall period luck would be adversely affected in the two years following its opening. Usually the year and month luck is favorable when there are favorable month and year numbers in the SW as this will compound the good luck. During the months when the numbers are inauspicious, there will be a slowdown in the business but it will be temporary.

For 1995 I discovered that the best months for the restaurant were the first three months and the last three months of the year. That was when the favorable 8, 7and 6 numbers flew into the SW.

The low months were the fourth, six and seventh months. Why? Because the annual number for SW in the year 1995 was 2, and when this is combined with the month numbers 2 and 5, the indications were inauspicious. When combined with 3 (as happened in the sixth month) it indicated quarrels and misunderstandings - perhaps between the partners, perhaps between the owner and the staff.

The **3/2** combination which often indicates quarrels and intense misunderstandings leading to problems, also feature prominently in the restaurant natal chart. **Note sectors NW and West** ! I thus predicted a falling out between the partners during this period. However because the main numerals are 8 and 9 , and because the SW had the double 7 combination, the restaurant's success would continue.

However there will be a great deal of unpleasantness in the midst of the restaurant's success.

CHAPTER
SEVEN

Flying
Star
Case
Studies

CASE
SEVEN

Flying Star Case Studies

CASE SEVEN
Because of a major reorganization in the company early in 1994, the entire sales department occupying the first floor of the company's building had to be **renovated**. This was to create additional rooms to house the newly appointed Regional Sales Manager and extra staff. The sales Director, Mr. Lee, was a friend of mine. He was concerned about the timing of the renovations so I invited him to bring his plans to discuss with me.

LAYOUT PLAN of FIRST FOOR SALES OFFICE
The sketch shows the plan of the first floor sales office. The entrance to the office is located in the Northwest . In 1994 the **grand Duke** is located in the West Northwest and in the year of 1995 it is located in the North North West. Now according to Flying Star , **one should never undertake any construction work in the sector housing the Grand Duke**.

Meanwhile the **location of the Three Killings in 1994 was the North.** Renovations may be done in the location opposite the three killings but not in the locations of the three killings itself i.e. in the North during 1994 (and in the West during 1995). Thus **in 1994, it was not advisable to disturb the two sectors - NW and North.** The consequences of doing so would be negative.

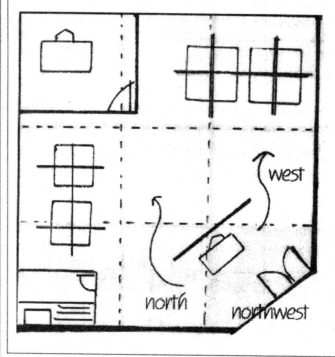

To determine whether either of the above two rules of feng shui was likely to be broken I studied the floor plan.

The main door was being moved from the Northwest to the North. This meant **the Grand Duke** would be disturbed. Also, the **3 killings** (North) was activated. I advised Mr. Lee to think twice before proceeding with the renovation.

CASE EIGHT

Datin Josephine had just finished redecorating her husbands family mansion in Jalan Kia Peng. Originally built during the mid 1950's the mansion had been renovated in **1974** when an additional wing had been added to the house. With both her children married, and her husbands company greatly expanded, Josephine wanted to increase the entertainment area at home. This involved breaking down some walls in the **South West** and **West** sectors. Josephine wanted to confirm that the renovation would not bring any bad feng shui for the family

THE AUSPICIOUS COMPASS DIRECTIONS

Datin Josephine has already determined that the main door of her house, located in the **South sector** and facing South represented her husbands most auspicious direction. And that the back door in the North also represented good luck for the family. As she was also an East group person like her husband, his directions were also auspicious for her. Both had benefited from the favorable location of their master bedroom in the East sector. The fortunes of her family had been smooth. Both the children had graduated held good jobs and married well. The family business continued to prosper, and both were in the best of health.

THE ANALYSIS

All spatial concepts had been adhered to and the family's feng shui luck was auspicious. The redecoration was limited to the SW and the West, and it had been ascertained that this would not disturb either the **Grand Duke** or the **3 Killings** . It would seem that the redecoration would not have any major negative effect on the feng shui of the family mansion. The only thing left to do was to check the existing Natal chart Lo Shu Under Period 6 with the new natal chart under period 7. The new chart looked like this.

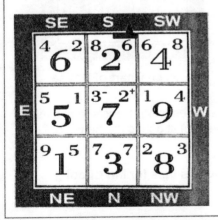

How would you advise Josephine ?

I would say DO NOT PROCEED. Look at the EAST sector with the **double 5** ! The Master bedroom is in the East. If the renovation had proceeded, the **double 5** would have caused either Josephine or her husband or both to become fatally ill. Also the middle grid has the 3/2 numerals indicating grave and unpleasant quarrels … Renovating would destroyed their happiness !

CHAPTER
SEVEN

Flying
Star
Case
Studies

CASE
NINE

Flying Star Case Studies

Seven

CASE NINE

Mr. Choo's company had been expanding at breakneck speed. With turnover doubling each year, Mr. Choo now required additional floor space and hire more people. Recently Mr. Choo was approached by the Chairman of a large conglomerate offering to buy out Mr. Choo's company in exchange for shares in one of the conglomerate's listed subsidiaries. Mr. Choo was torn between wanting to cash in and wanting to continue building his business.

Mr. Choo is personally knowledgeable about feng shui, and he had been having long discussions with Mr. Yap about flying star feng shui. He decided to analyze his **time luck** for the present 7 period, as he was convinced that knowing what kind of luck awaited him would greatly assist him in his decision.

We studied the Natal charts of both his house and his office which are presented here for comparison and analysis. These charts had shown me why he had done so well in the past few years. Consider :

- In the office he sits in the **Northeast** corner, and the entrance to his office is located in the **Southwest.**
- At home his bedroom is located in the **West** sector and the entrance to the house is also located in the West.

Natal chart of Office

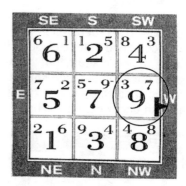

Natal Chart of House

The numbers indicated in the two chart offer clues to Mr. Choo's feng shui luck. Since both the office and the house were built during the period of 7, the center numbers of both charts is 7.

Both charts indicate very auspicious luck for Mr. Choo!

CASE NINE contd …

THE OFFICE NATAL CHART

In the office, Mr. Choo's room location in the Northeast enjoys the **formidable luck of the double 7.** It is an excellent indication of wealth coming to him during this period 7. In addition the entrance to the office also has the siang sin star 1 which coincides with the main numeral of the NE sector. **1** is also an indicator of prosperity

THE HOUSE NATAL CHART

In the house, Mr. Choo's bedroom and main entrance are both located in the **West sector**. Once again the secondary stars have flown around the Lo Shu and settled in most auspicious manner for Mr. Choo. In the West sector, the two secondary stars **7 and 3 add up to 10** – an excellent indicator of wealth luck. Because the West is also his personalized auspicious sector the 3 + 7 combination is extremely propitious for Mr. Choo. Also the 7 siang sin is an excellent water star !

CONCLUSION

It is obvious that Mr. Choo's business luck is very good during the period of 7. His prosperity star is definitely shinning! According to feng shui manuals, when this indication is given, it does not matter what Mr. Choo decides.

Whatever he does – whether he sells out or not, he will prosper. Incidentally, Mr. Choo is a West person, and his house is good for him based on his own auspicious directions as well. But his office luck add weight to his good fortune. The **double 7** combination is especially good during this period. To sell out would mean giving up the office – so it might be better to carry on.

POST SCRIPT

Mr. Choo (name disguised) did accept the offer from the conglomerate. That was five years ago !

But he kept 20% of the company and accepted an offer to stay on as the chief executive officer of the company. He was also made a director on the main board. Meanwhile the shares in the main company which he accepted as consideration for selling 80% of his company has appreciated in value by nearly 300 %.

Today Mr. Choo is a very happy man. By tapping into the connections of the conglomerate, Mr.Choo's business is growing faster than ever. He has however kept his old office, declining an offer to move into the conglomerate's plush new head quarters.

CHAPTER
SEVEN

Flying
Star
Case
Studies

CASE
TEN

Flying Star Case Studies

CASE TEN

Mr. and Mrs. Ling bought a semi-detached house in Taman Tun Dr Ismail in December 1994, but since moving in, the children had been in and out of hospital, first with one thing then another. At work Mr. Ling had been having problems with his boss. Mrs. Ling suspected that the feng shui of the house was giving her family problems. She asked us to check.

When we analyzed the Ling's new home we discovered that their main front door was in a direction that represented Mr. Ling's worst direction (his Chueh Ming total loss direction !). The Natal chart also indicated that the main door was suffering from a configuration of extremely inauspicious numbers. Obviously something would have to be done about the door. Let's take a look at the feng shui of the Ling's home. First the layout.

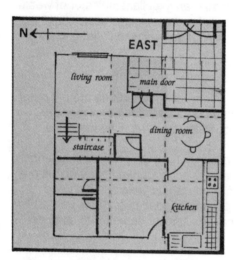

Note the main door is located in the East and facing East. Unfortunately for Mr. Ling, he is a west person and the direction East actually represents **Chueh Ming** direction (please refer to my book Pa Kua Lo Shu Feng Shui for more on this compass school theory of feng shui).

This new house seems most unsuitable for him No wonder he is having problems at work. There is worse to come, as we shall see when we draw up the natal chart of the house

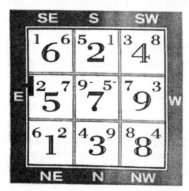

This is a period 7 house with its door located in the East sector. The natal chart indicates grave ill fortune for the house due to the numbers in the east sector (shaded).
The **5** main numeral is an indicator of grave illness and bad luck, and this gets compounded by the chor sin **2**.

CASE TEN contd …

I advised that the location and direction of the main door be changed. . Referring to the natal chart, and superimposing it onto the house layout, one can see that the house feng shui could be substantially improved if the front door was **moved to the Northeast** sector, facing northeast. By changing the orientation and location of the front door, both flying star and Eight Mansions feng shui luck improved for Mr. Ling. At the same time, by removing the door away from the illness bringing **5 of the East** sector and substituting it for the auspicious number **1 of the Northeast** the feng shui of the house improved.

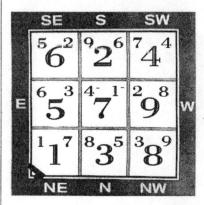

The Lo Shu grid on the left is the new natal chart of Mr. Ling's new house with the **main door moved to the Northeast.** Since renovation work was involved, it was necessary to ensure that neither the Northeast nor the East were taboo directions for the year i.e. that any renovation work did not arouse either the Grand Duke Jupiter or set off the Three Killings! A quick check indicated the taboo directions in 1994 were NW and North. Mr. Ling could thus proceed.

The New Natal Chart has the lucky star 7 as the siang sin and the lucky star 1 as the chor sin in the sector of the main door. The main numeral of the NE is also 1. Thus all three numbers are auspicious.

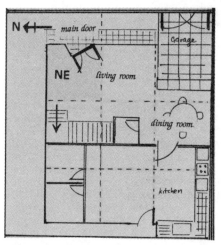

The layout of the house now looks like this. Please note the direction of the main door. It has been placed at an angle to face NE to capture Mr. Ling's best sheng chi direction. Notice also that the inauspicious sector is **Southeast** with the **deadly 2/5** combination. This is occupied by the garage and thus does not harm the family.

Frequently asked Questions

Thunder repeated - the image of shock brings success
The superior man sets his life in order
And examines himself

**From the I CHING on the
Hexagram Chen – the Arousing**

Which method of Feng shui is the best ?

There is no such thing as the best method to use. Basically all authentic methods and techniques of feng shui are inter connected through the use of the same source knowledge and symbols. The differences lie in the emphasis on symbols are more important, and in the interpretations. My advice is to learn a few very fundamental methods of Compass formula techniques (of which Flying Star is one) and then to also master the practical applications of Landscape and Symbolic feng shui. Then when you are trying to implement a particular recommendation let yourself be guided by your own judgement on the solutions you come up with. When in doubt always go for the method that will offer you protection from bad feng shui.

If there is a conflict between Flying star and the Directions formula which method should I follow ?

When you are confronted with two seemingly contradictory pieces of advice on the placement and direction of doors and sitting and sleeping locations always select the solution that will cause you to be protected from bad feng shui. The Masters are very clear about the need to always be protected from bad killing breath, the shar chi. This is because shar chi is believed to have the power to dominate and overcome the auspicious sheng chi. Thus when confronted with indecision stay defensive and you won't go wrong. Remember that all authentic feng shui formulas always work, so it is always a question of your preference what you want to achieve.

Is this book sufficiently comprehensive about Flying Star feng shui or do I need to go deeper ?

It is up to you how advanced you wish to be in your practice. For the basic practitioner who wishes to be alerted to particularly bad periods brought on by the flying stars this book is more than sufficient.

Frequently asked Questions

How do I superimpose the Lo Shu grid over a house plan which has an irregular shape ?

Think of your house plans in terms of "missing corners" and "extended" corners. Try to include as much of your covered areas as possible and then treat all those spaces that you cannot include into the grid as extended corners. Treat these extended areas as strengthening the corner from which it extended. See the sketch here. The bits in white are missing corners. The extension strengthens the corner from which it extended. What applies to the corner applies to the extension as well.

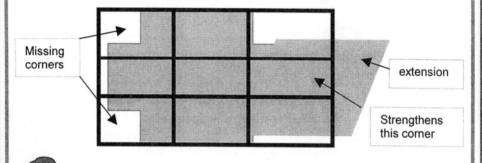

Missing corners

extension

Strengthens this corner

are there other ways of demarcating the compass sectors of a house ? Does it always have to be a grid ?

Yes because the whole basis of Flying Star is the Lo Shu grid. That is the foundation of the Formula itself. However there are some very good practitioners who use a different method. They use the circular compass to demarcate the house space by degrees as shown here and on the cover.

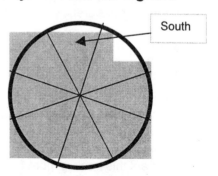

South

Frequently asked Questions

If I live in the SOUTHERN HEMISPHERE do I need to consider north as south, and south as north ?
No it is completely unnecessary to change the compass directions when you are using the Flying Star computations to examine good and bad luck periods for the different sectors of your home. In fact if you do change the direction around you will run into severe problems caused by wrong implementation. **Please do not change the directions.** I know that certain feng shui Practitioners who have done exactly this in Australia who caused their clients to go bankrupt so please do be careful. Feng shui is a very ancient practice and when you change the direction around you are in effect rewriting the source books and also changing the sequence of the Pa Kua trigrams upon which ALL of feng shui is based.

But I have read that the winds in say Australia are different and that because the equator is to the north … it is wrong to regard south as being the element of fire. To us south represents cold ….

It is here that the basis of the misinformation originated. Many people speculate that Feng shui considers South to be the place of fire because the equator lies to the south of China.. this is not so. **The reason South is symbolic of fire comes from the TRIGRAM Li** which is placed south in the Later Heaven arrangement of the Pa Kua. Li is the trigram of fire and hence the south is said to be symbolic of fire. If you change it around you would be using a Pa Kua arrangement of Trigrams that has no basis in the feng shui lineage. And besides … winds are not cold or hot simply from the directions north or south .. the temperature of all winds are affected by localized weather conditions. Winds come from all directions. It is not correct to surmise that the basis of feng shui is wind direction alone… and finally please remember that compass directions are merely a tool for interpreting the symbols that play a part in feng shui terminology and recommendations. No single factor is all-important. If you change directions everything goes out of sync and you will be making grave errors of implementation.

Frequently asked Questions

How do I know which subsection my main door is actually facing ? How important is it to be exact ?

Actually it is absolutely vital to be very exact in your compass readings since the exact direction which your main door is facing determines the flight path mode of the siang sin and chor sin stars. So if your main door is facing NORTH you must determine whether it is in the first, second or third subsection of North... and the same for all the other 8 main directions. The best way to determine this is to take a reading and then use this Table here to determine the exact subsection of direction.

	Bearing °		Bearing °		Bearing
South 1	157.5 –172.5	South 2	172.5-187.5	South 3	187.5-202.5
North 1	337.5 –352.5	North 2	352.5-007.5	North 3	007.5-022.5
East 1	067.5-082.5	East 2	082.5 –097.5	East 3	097.5-112.5
West 1	247.5-262.5	West 2	262.5-277.5	West 3	277.5-292.5
Southwest 1	202.5-217.5	Southwest 2	217.5-232.5	Southwest 3	232.5-247.5
Southeast 1	112.5-127.5	Southeast 2	127.5-142.5	Southeast 3	142.5-157.5
Northeast 1	022.5-037.5	Northeast 2	037.5-052.5	Northeast 3	052.5-067.5
Northwest 1	292.5-307.5	Northwest 2	307.5-322.5	Northwest 3	322.5-352.5

You will note that the compass directions take 360 degrees to go all the way round and there is a total of 24 sectors of sub directions and each subsection measures 15 degrees. This allows you to be very accurate in your compass measurements.

from where should I take these directions ?

I always advise that directions should be taken from just inside the main door looking out. What you want to know is what direction the door faces looking out, and not looking in. To be really accurate I also advise that three readings be made since this will take care of any energy field caused around the door area which could cause the reading to be inaccurate. If you take three readings and they are all different (bound to be) use the average of the three readings.

Frequently asked Questions

If I have more than one main door, which should I use for computing the flying star natal chart ?

In feng shui the main door is defined as the door which you use the most frequently to get in and out of your house. This is the conventional definition for main door. However there are a couple of variations to this guideline. Some Masters say that the main door is the door that faces the main road, so that even if that is not the door you use the most frequently that should be the door you use to compute the natal chart. Yet other Masters say that the main door is the biggest door in the house. Thus those of you who have French windows that open right to the floor level will have to decide whether to use this door as the main door for purposes of computing the natal chart. As for my views I prefer to go with the conventional definition which is the door I use the most frequently.

Is there a different way of analyzing the luck of houses that are long and narrow e.g. link houses ?

Again some very advanced Masters look at a house and if they see that it is long and narrow with only two rooms making up the width of the house, what they do is "**drop the center vertical grid**" for purposes of demarcating the sectors. This means that the sectors north, south and center gets dropped in the analysis. And where the width of the house is made up of only one room than they drop the two vertical grids by the sides and use only the center panel of three grids for analysis. This is illustrated in the sketches below:

This panel of grids drops off and is not considered when there are two rooms to the width of a long narrow house

The two side panels drop off and are not considered when there is only one room in the width of the house.

Frequently asked Questions

Can I practice Flying Star exclusively and not worry about the other methods of feng shui ?

In Hong Kong most people observe only the From School feng shui of green dragon white tiger and flying star. They consider this to be sufficient. In Taiwan Flying star feng shui is not very popular since they practice mainly Eight Mansions formula and the From School.

Thus it really depends on what you want to do and which aspects of feng shui you wish to focus on. This is because feng shui is a practice that has great depth and breadth of meanings.

For me personally I have found that it is not necessary to use all the methods all the time. It is also not possible to get one's feng shui absolutely perfect according to all the schools of feng shui. For this reason I frequently remind everyone not to worry when they notice something wrong with their feng shui. Most of the time there is an inexpensive way of reducing the problem, and even of dissolving the cause of bad energy completely.

Do I need to get a FENG SHUI Master in to calculate my flying star natal chart for my home ?

No, you do not need a special feng shui consultant to work it out for you. Please note that in Chapter Three I have calculated the Natal chart of all PERIOD 7 houses. If your house was built or renovated any time from 1984 to the current time one of these charts will be your Natal chart. All you need to find out which chart is yours, just check the direction of your main door and having found the correct natal chart, read the chapter on meanings of numbers and the chapter on the five elements to give yourself a reading. You can also use the time charts to investigate the luck of your house for this coming year, for the next year and so forth… I have also given solutions for the incidence of bad stars. So armed with this book, you really are ready to give yourself a proper and correct flying star reading. So good luck to you !!!